UNCOVERING THE RIGHT

ON CAMPUS

PRODUCED BY THE STAFF OF THE CENTER
FOR CAMPUS ORGANIZING

PROJECT COORDINATOR
Rich Cowan

RESEARCH AND EDITING
Nari Rhee, Dalya Massachi,
Michael Kennedy, Ami Roeder, Nicole
Newton, and Harley Gambill

DESIGN AND LAYOUT
Ben Leon, Ami Roeder, and Jim Sheehy

distributed by:
Center for Campus Organizing
P.O. Box 748
Cambridge, MA 02142
(617) 354-9363

LA
227.4
.U63
1997

publisher:
Public Search, Inc.
P.O. Box 54038
Houston, TX 77254-0381

printed in the U.S.A.

isbn: 0-945210-07-8
Library of Congress
Catalogue Card Number: 96-066261

Cover: Student free speech movement demonstration in Sproul Plaza, University of California at Berkeley, 1964. One conservative student opposed to the movement is holding the sign "University Students for Law and Order." Photo by Ron Riesterer; design by Ben Leon, Rich Cowan, and Tatsu Ikeda.

Table of Contents

Acknowledgements

We would like to express our appreciation to all of the people who donated time to the production of this book, including all the staff and interns at the Center for Campus Organizing. Besides the authors and editors, the following is an incomplete list of individuals and organizations that helped us in completing this guide:

Amy Lang, Amy Ledoux, Barry Mehler, Beth Daley, Bob Anderson, Chip Berlet, Dina Carreras, Don Hazen, Doug Calvin, Ellen Messer-Davidow, Fred Clarkson, Hans Riemer, Heather McLeod, Howard Ehrlich, Ivan Frishberg, Jadwiga Sebrechts, Janet Shenk, Jean Caiani, John K. Wilson, John Peck, Kerry Lobel, Kit Boyce, Loretta Ross, Lou Wolf, Mary Mitchell, Maureen McRae, Michelle Persard, Miles Seligman, Mitchell Grotch, Nan Aron, Niels Berger, Noam Chomsky, Nova Clarke, Pamela Wilson, Pete Self, Peter Hannan, Rachel Egen, Reginald Wilson, Sally Covington, Sid Shapiro, Stephanie Arellano, Tatsu Ikeda, Taylor Root, and Terry Laban

We'd also like to thank the following organizations (again an incomplete list) for helping with graphics and research assistance:

Catholics for a Free Choice, *In These Times*, People for the American Way, National Gay and Lesbian Task Force, National Student News Service, National Council for Research on Women, the US Student Association, Political Research Associates, Speak Out!, Student Press Law Center, *The Gainesville Iguana,* US Public Interest Research Groups

Foundations who contributed to CCO's research into the campus Right: The Arca Foundation, Boehm Foundation, Funding Exchange, Haymarket People's Fund, HKH Foundation, List Foundation, Ms. Foundation for Women, and the Shefa Fund

Preface

To the Reader:

When we first announced that we were getting into the business of examining the Right, some of our supporters were curious. Why spend time on opposition research rather than focus on our own organizing?

Actually, that's what we had been doing, but something was going awry. Our contacts reported a growing student distaste for political involvement or even discussion of social issues. The "anti-PC" wave which swept from coast to coast seemed to have left an indelible imprint on campus culture. Students were confused about their personal values of "freedom," "justice," and even "peace." Any time a progressive group did something effective, groups dedicated to "individual rights" and "ordered liberty" were ready to discredit and marginalize the activists involved. These reactionary efforts seemed to be well organized and efficiently coordinated, but no national progressive groups were monitoring or countering this situation.

So we secured funding for our project in January of 1993, and began our research. We needed to find out what was really happening on college campuses, so we asked hundreds of student activists all over the country to share their experiences. We also contacted the new forces that had cropped up on the right and collected their literature. We scoured libraries, made lists, and followed the money trail. The puzzle began to come together.

In the spring of 1994, under the name "University Conversion Project," we sounded the alarm by exposing the hidden and not-so-hidden agendas of the campus Right in an early edition of this guide. But the true wake-up call came that fall when Right-wing forces took over both houses of Congress. In this volatile political situation, we began a second round of research in the summer of 1995 and made plans for this new Guide.

Our cumulative research efforts revealed a network of over a dozen national groups with annual budgets ranging from $160,000 to $5,000,000 who were coordinating most conservative campus activities.

This network funds over 60 Right-wing campus publications reaching almost a million students. It conducts seminars, sponsors lectures, organizes training programs for young conservatives, and even provides legal and financial support for students fighting progressive groups or campus administrations. Its faculty supporters include most of the professors speaking out against sexual harassment policies and multicultural curricula. Its spokespeople include Bill Bennett, Jeanne Kirkpatrick, Phyllis Schlafly, and Dinesh D'Sousa. Its goals include, among others, a return to "family values," the defunding of Public Interest Research Groups and the US Student Association, and the defeat of "radical environmentalists" on campus.

Universities ought to provide an environment both on campus and in the community that respects a diversity of peoples, ideas, and circumstances — and in no way threatens the well being of any member of that community or their full participation in any facet of society. This goal is rooted in both the historic ideals of academia and the struggles of progressive students, faculty, and communities at large to bring those ideals to life. The funding provided to the campus Right, and the ideas coupled with such support, are part of a concerted campaign to end this tradition.

We present this booklet with two goals in mind:

1) to inform local activists who might otherwise be isolated or silenced by this conservative backlash. Once we know the facts and the funding behind such organizations as the Intercollegiate Studies Institute, Young America's Foundation, and the Center for the Study of Popular Culture, their actions can be more effectively countered.

2) to help those outside the university balance the media-generated images of "tenured radicals," "lower standards," and "political correctness" — images which serve to justify massive cutbacks in higher education.

We at the Center for Campus Organizing are impressed by the energy and spirit present on the Right. These individuals are steadfast in their beliefs, and their generous funding produces a healthy organization with more appeal to many concerned students than a disorganized and financially constrained "left" group.

The damage wrought by these groups should not be underestimated. Where their religious fundamentalism, free-market ideology, and rampant individualism blinds them to participatory, democratic solutions, they may resign themselves to quasi-fascist ones. For example, Third Millennium proposes more prisons and police to address crime without recognizing the role of neo-liberal economic policies in displacing millions of people, thereby rendering them expendable. Many Right-wing activities occupy the margins of "legality"; in this way hate groups are able claim legitimacy for their acts of open intimidation and harrassment. For instance, anti-Semitic groups contend that publishing Holocaust denial ads in campus newspapers is only an exercise of the freedom of the press, when in fact, such ads have incited cases of anti-Semitic violence.

But fear not. Despite the tens of millions of dollars spent by the Right to turn back the clock to the 50s, they are not winning our generation. Most students want more money spent on education, not war; most women are not abandoning their careers; and multiculturalism and the gay rights movement are gaining ground. This process depends on our participation. Together, we helped to stall the onslaught of the Newt Gingrich revolution. Together, we can derail the Right's attempts to divide us, and give new direction to future progressive movements.

—*The Editors*

Cambridge, MA, June 1997

FRONT LINES:

CONSERVATIVE BACKLASH ON COLLEGE CAMPUSES

Kit Boyce/ In These Times

The Big Picture

Rich Cowan and Nari Rhee

We have resisted the official dogmas of radical feminism. We have done the same thing with regard to gay and lesbian liberation... we have resisted the fad of Afrocentrism. We have not fallen into the clutches of the multi-culturalists. We recognize that Western culture, so-called, is in fact a universal culture.
— John Silber, president of Boston University, in his annual *Report to the Trustees,* April 1993

Opposition to education programs has not just been a passing fancy for conservative politicians; it has been a centerpiece of the Right's agenda. In 1991, President George Bush devoted a major address to denouncing "political correctness" in higher education. In 1995, Newt Gingrich won approval in Congress for a $10 billion cut in student aid, while newly elected governors trimmed education and expanded prisons. Every major Republican presidential candidate in 1996 said he would abolish the Department of Education.

Why is the Right so opposed to education? The reasons are apparent once we define what we mean by "Right Wing." For the purposes of this guide, we will define the Right as "those who want to limit democracy" — individuals or groups who want to limit participation and preserve privilege in our society, who believe corporate dollars should have more weight than people's votes. We will also define the Right as "those who want to limit pluralism" — individuals or groups dedicated to ensuring that the ideas, language, culture, and values of white, English-speaking, heterosexual, Christians have a monopoly in our society.

While there are individuals who qualify as "Right-wing" by this definition in both the Republican and the Democratic party, the Right's power as a political force depends on unified leadership that exists outside either party. This leadership today is a not-so-easy alliance between economic conservatives (big business), and Christian Conservatives (fundamentalists and white nationalists). While these factions disagree on some issues, such as free trade and banning abortion, they agree on attacking government. By reducing the government's role in regulating commerce, providing a safety net, and advancing the status of women and people of color, more people will be dependent on the church and the "private sector."

Given this definition, the Right's virulent opposition to education is more easily understood. Education gives people the ability to learn more about the world, make decisions for themselves, and participate in the democratic process. And higher education — especially public higher education — is a democratic institution which competes with the hierarchical Church and corporate America. The battle over what is taught in higher education, who gets access to it, and the way in which students are acculturated on college campuses is both symbolically and practically a battle for the hegemony of the society at large.

This guide focuses on right-wing activities *on campus* because the Right has decided that its message will be most effective if it comes not only from conservative politicians but also from within the halls of academia. When working within a campus, the Right aligns itself with traditionally conservative elitist forces within the university, and focuses on "wedge issues" that divide liberal opinion. On campuses, creationism would be a hard sell. But free-market economics, attacks on affirmative action, and opposition to codes regulating hate crime are effective.

Backed by over $4 million each year from conservative foundations, this strategy is very effective at diminishing the role of universities as a democratizing force in our society. Wherever academia gives students exposure to alternative political and economic ideas, the Right is there to see that traditional ideas are reinforced. Many of the conservative students and professors cultivated and trained by the Right go on to fill leadership positions within the Right-wing movement.

★ ★ ★ ★ ★

In the past three years, the campus Right-wing has undergone some significant changes. The Madison Center and its network of student newspapers was absorbed by the Intercollegiate Studies Institute, which moved to Delaware. The First Amendment Coalition was absorbed by the Individual Rights Foundation.

Support for economic conservatism on campus declined as a result of Republican attacks on education spending and activism against the Contract with America. The president of the conservative Young Americas Foundation took notice, writing in 1995 that "I have never seen the left more galvanized and focussed [sic] than they have become since the fall of 1994." Conservative organizations found that the charge of "political correctness" no longer carried the punch it once had. The

Right reacted by increasing efforts to organize conservative alumni and trustees, through groups such as the National Alumni Forum.

Meanwhile, Christian conservatives gained in campus influence. And the Religious Right successfully manipulated the court system to win school funding for religious propaganda at the expense of funding for progressive organizations, through the court cases of *Rosenberger v. University of Virginia* and *Smith v. Regents* in California.

Attacks against marginalized groups, minority student associations, and ethnic studies and women's studies programs gained momentum. Howard Ehrlich wrote in *Campus Ethnoviolence: A Research Review,* "The opponents of 'political correctness' argue for their own freedom from bigotry [by redefining] as bigots the advocates of ethnic and feminist studies and multiculturalism in curricula." In using this strategy, the Right has attempted to appropriate the terms "civil rights" and "feminism" as part of initiatives to abolish programs which serve people of color and women.

The Right has also tried to win widespread legitimacy for such efforts through bigotry disguised as "science." This is not new: we saw this with nineteenth century eugenicists and later, Nazi scientists. In 1995, the argument that that I.Q. is an important determinant of one's social and economic class swept across the US with the publication of *The Bell Curve.* This kind of scholarship continues to enjoy a wide audience, fueling a bipartisan war against the poor in which even Democrats may express enthusiastic support for welfare reform.

Finally, the publications apparatus of the Right continued to regurgitate the same myths to undermine progressive activists and discredit the power of the academic voice on social and economic issues:

- *With the end of the Cold War, the Right has demobilized.* Energy directed by conservative groups against the Soviet Union has been redeployed domestically, with the universities as a primary target.
- *Campuses are "hotbeds of the Left."* The millions of corporate and military dollars poured into universities for research contracts and professorships show that they are not dominions of "leftist" activity and "tenured radicals." Socially-relevant topics and perspectives may be included as a token gesture to cover for corporate and military ties.
- *Political Correctness represents a "crisis in education."* The real crisis is budget-slashing. Programs and scholarships designed to make higher education relevant and accessible to people of color and lower income students are on the chopping block. The Right discredits inclusive higher education as "PC" to reinforce growing class stratification and institutionalized racism within higher education.

- *Right-wing campus newspapers tend to be more "rational."* Claiming to have cornered the market on "rationality," these papers are notorious for shady facts and out-of-context quotes. Some are used as personal slam-sheets and self-promotion tools for writers seeking a job with a New Right think-tank after college (i.e., Dinesh D'Souza).
- *Freedom of speech automatically protects hate-mongers.* Legally speaking, threatening verbal behavior is not the same thing as freedom of speech. The issues are complex when people use demeaning or harassing language against others.
- *"The Left" tons of on-campus funding for multiculturalism, feminism, gay and lesbian issues, etc.* Sometimes the administration will fund only those groups that help attract tuition-paying students and meet affirmative action goals. The "identity" groups are seldom those groups who question the racism and sexism of campus programs, or adopt a multi-issue or anti-capitalist perspective.

★ ★ ★ ★ ★

A dangerous fallacy held by some activists is that paying attention to the Right Wing is a waste of time. If we wish to do more than preach to the converted, we must strategize about how ideas spread by the Right affect the response of new people we are trying to organize. What tactics are we using that worked before Right-wing groups got organized, but which no longer work today? We encourage all groups to reevaluate their strategy to address the Right's presence.

The right's goals are well understood. They want to siphon off popular political energy and prevent the development of the movements for democracy and equality. How can we encourage members of our communities to see through the facade of "populist" groups who use coached tactics and glossy brochures extolling "freedom," even as they take orders from their corporate bosses? How can we free ourselves from the influence of propaganda campaigns designed to convince us that racism, sexism, and environmental problems have been fixed; that if we are queer we are sick; that if we sell out we'll get ahead?

Organizing can still succeed. The battle to save student aid of 1995 and 1996 demonstrated the power of collective action, and that when exposed for all to see, the Right-wing agenda is very unpopular. However, the Right remains strong. This publication offers tools to better understand the struggle that we face, so that we can continue making our campuses useful places to learn about both ourselves and those around us. We can't afford to allow a backlash to obstruct our path.

Intolerance on Campus

by the CCO Staff

It seems almost inconceivable, after years of struggle against discrimination and racial prejudice in the U.S., that a candidate for the highest office in the nation could openly consort with bigots. Yet during the 1996 presidential campaign, one of Pat Buchanan's campaign chairs, Larry Pratt, was revealed to have addressed meetings of White Supremacists.

Some people reacted to this news with disgust and anger. But among a sizable portion of the population, it seemed that Buchanan's message was amplified and energized, rather than muted, by the revelation.

We live in a time when politicians build careers on singling out the weak and the disenfranchised as targets of widespread derision and anger, when blame is the elixir for the problems facing our society and scapegoating becomes a kind of public therapy. California's downward spiral is the fault of immigrants. Welfare mothers created the deficit. The 1960s frayed the moral fiber of the country. African–American men perpetrate all crime. Gays have destroyed family values.

With anger comes violence. According to the *Race Relations Reporter*, race-related incidents in the US climbed by 20 percent in 1995. The FBI reported that hate crime activities rose at the time of the O.J. Simpson trial verdict, and there were more reported hate crime incidents in October 1995 — the month of the verdict — than in any other month of the year. In their yearly audit of anti-Semitic incidents around the country, the Anti–Defamation League reported 1,843 reported in 1995. These included 1,116 acts of personal assault and harassment and 727 acts of vandalism. And hate crimes are disproportionately committed by the most impressionable members of our society: young people. A report by the Southern Poverty Law Center indicates that youths under the age of 21 — about a third of the population — make up half of all hate crime offenders.

College campuses, supposedly a haven of rational thought, are no exception. Below is a list of incidents of racism, anti–Semitism, and intolerance against members of different communities on campuses. In no way is this a complete list; we encourage you to document and research such episodes on your own campus, make them known, and organize to prevent them from happening again.

White Supremacy / Anti-Semitism

During 1992–1996, white supremacists increased campus activity. The White Supremacy Party began recruiting at **Bradley University** in Peoria, Illinois. At the **University of Florida-Gainesville** and **Temple University** in Philadelphia, White Student Unions won university recognition. In addition, David Duke was endorsed by a fraternity at **Southeastern University** in Louisiana and by **Louisiana Northwestern University** Young Republicans.

University of New Mexico: Flyers for Baha'i National Day Against Racism were defaced with rubber stamp imprints of a red swastika with a skull pierced by two swords and the words "Racism: Pride and Loyalty."

University of New Mexico: A swastika was painted on a mural in the student union building.

University of New Mexico: A sticker with a swastika and the words "White power" was found in the Humanities building.

University of New Mexico: A racist and anti-Semitic flyer was distributed throughout campus.

Cornell, Duke, Northeastern Illinois U, Rutgers, U Michigan-Ann Arbor, U Miami, U Central Florida, U Georgia, Illinois State U, Columbia College, Purdue U, Queens College, Hofstra U, U Akron, Ohio State U and Penn State U: "Holocaust Revisionists" placed a full-page ad in student newspapers at these universities questioning the deaths of millions in Nazi concentration camps. (Note: the internet newsgroup on Holocaust denial, "alt.revisionism", is widely available at most campuses on the Internet.)

University of Miami: Three incidents occurred in the wake of a Holocaust-denial advertisement: 1) the Science Center was vandalized with "Fuck the Jews" graffiti, 2) Hillel received an anti-Semitic phone call, 3) the President of the Jewish Student Union received an anti-Semitic postcard.

University of Miami: The words "racism is good" and a swastika were painted in a men's bathroom on campus.

University of Connecticut-Storrs: Anti-Semitic and anti-Black graffiti was found in three locations in a dorm, including "Fuck the Jews" and swastikas.

University of Minnesota-St. Paul: A mannequin head burned black with a swastika painted on its forehead was hanged by a noose from a stairwell in a residence hall.

De Paul University: A swastika and "Kill the Jew Bitch" were written on the door of a residence hall advisor.

Northwestern University: A swastika and "Nazis live" were written on the door of a Jewish student.

Michigan State University-E. Lansing: A rock with a swastika and a note, "Jews will die for the Fatherland," was thrown into an administration building.

Howard University, University of Florida, Southern Illinois University, Trenton State University, New York University, CCNY-York College, University of Wisconsin-Milwaukee: Khalid Abdul Muhammad made anti-Semitic statements in a speech on campus.

Central Connecticut State University, Hofstra University, Westchester County Community College, University of Wisconsin-Milwaukee: Leonard Jeffries made anti-Semitic statements in a speech on campus.

Student Fees

Public Interest Research Groups (PIRGs) and the US Student Association (USSA) have both endured numerous attacks, starting in the 1980's, on their collection of funds through student fees. Young Americans for Freedom, Accuracy in Academia, and College Republicans have disrupted their conferences, resorted to name-calling in student publications and actively promoted student government candidates opposed to PIRGs and USSA.

University of California: In early 1993, the State Supreme Court *(Smith v. Regents)* ruled that student fees could not be used to support groups with which students ideologically disagreed. This will effectively limit the number of controversial ideas brought to campus by activities fees.

St. Louis University: Backed by the conservative campus organization Eagle Forum Collegians, students were able to defund the Missouri Public Interest Research Group (MoPIRG).

Northern Arizona University: Again with the help of the Eagle Forum Collegians, students were able to defund the campus United States Student Association (USSA) chapter.

University of Wisconsin-Madison: The Wisconsin Student Association (WSA) was disbanded in the summer of 1993 after the debate over student fee allocation rendered the student government ineffective. Writers from the campus right-wing newspaper won many seats in the student government and were able to topple it with the "Kill the WSA Party," headed by a student identifying with Rush Limbaugh and his attack on "Femi-Nazis."

University of Wisconsin-Madison: The UW Greens, WisPIRG, Campus Women's Center and the Lesbian, Gay, Bisexual Center were targeted for defunding in a "First Amendment" lawsuit underwritten by the Phoenix, Arizona-based Alliance Defense Fund, an organization founded by conservative Christian leaders Bill Bright (Campus Crusade for Christ) and James Dobson (Focus on the Family).

University of Virginia: In a case decided in the Supreme Court (*Rosenberger v. Rector and Visitors of the University of Virginia*) in early July 1995, Ron Rosenberger was granted access to the annual student fees collected from those attending UVA to fund the publication of his Christian evangelical magazine, *Wide Awake*. Many believe that this decision may be the beginning of the end of church-state separation.

Harassment of Faculty

The following are incidents where faculty experienced harassment based on race, sex, sexual orientation, and religious beliefs.

Bethel College: After 21 years of teaching, Kenneth Gowdy was fired for voicing support (outside of class) for life-long homosexual relationships.

Brigham Young University: Cecilia Konchar Farr, Asst. Professor of English, was criticized by officials for speaking at a 1992 abortion rights rally, even after clearly stating she was not speaking for BYU. Without warning, she was fired in June 1993 for "inferior teaching and scholarship."

National Women's Studies Association: The Academic Discrimination Task Force, started in the early 1980's, has received dozens of reports from faculty members on acts of intimidation including lesbian-bashing on e-mail, physical assault on an Indian department chair, and sexual harassment of a lesbian tenure candidate.

South Alabama University: A Jewish faculty member found a note in his campus mailbox declaring, "Death to Jews — That means you..."

Clark University: A campus security officer received in the mail a picture of herself that had appeared in a newspaper, defaced with the handwritten words, "You lesbian — kike — Jew yid."

Northwestern University: A Jewish professor received a threatening phone call.

This was published on a poster by a Right-wing student newspaper, prompting a lawsuit from Simspson's creator Matt Groenig (courtesy of FAIR)

The following are incidents where students experienced harassment based on race, sex, sexual orientation, religious beliefs.

Willamette University: The words "go home nigger" were scrawled on the door of an African-American student's dorm room. Two lesbian women were spat upon and called "fucking dykes."

University of New Orleans: Two youths were arrested for making obscene phone calls to students, including threats of violence against persons thought to be gay.

University of South Florida: More than twenty calls were left on the USF Gay/Lesbian/ Bisexual Coalition's answering machine with anti-gay statements and threats, including "Ten homosexuals, five lesbians and two bisexuals will die in Tampa, Florida during the month of April." The student responsible for making this call was suspended from the school for two years.

St. Mary's College of Maryland: Two incidents have occurred in which a student group, Society for the Betterment of Campus, "called out" presumably gay Residence Assistants and student government personnel as being "unfit" for their jobs.

Villanova University: Having been denied university recognition for a gay/lesbian/bisexual student group, students created and advertised a voice mail phone list, through which they received several harassing phone calls.

Villanova University: At the annual Take Back The Night march, marchers were verbally harassed by men in the dorms at several points along the route.

Morehouse College: Verbal abuse against gays and lesbians led the Dean of Student Affairs to cancel gay programming and ban letters to the campus newspaper on the subject.

Saddleback College: The president of Black United Students, after being nominated for Homecoming King, received a flyer in his mailbox that said, in letters cut-out from a newspaper and pieced together ransom-style: "Niggers Are Monkeys Not Kings."

Tufts University: Writers for the campus alternative student newspaper were personally attacked. Physical assaults, hate mail, flyering, and faked correspondence have also plagued alternative publications at the **University of Florida-Gainesville, UC Davis, Dartmouth, and Carnegie-Mellon**.

...and many more. A list of all incidents where students or faculty have been harrassed on their campuses would take up more space than we can allocate here. However, if you have experienced or witnessed any kind of verbal or physical intimidation and harrassment, please notify the proper authorities on your campus, and pressure your administration to make statistics on hate crime publicly available. Students themselves can take an active part in this process by distributing information about hate crime on campus if the authorities do not comply. Universities generally do not assume responsibility for reporting this information, but we hope you will.

Anti-Gay Ads

by Nicole Newton

As of 1996, gay, lesbians, bisexual and transgendered people still do not have constitutional protection from discrimination in the Unites States. Conservatives distort this fact by claiming that the fight for equal rights is a battle for "special rights." Dr. Mark Draper, former Executive Director of the Right-wing think-tank Accuracy in Academia (AIA), states in his article "Hooray for Homophobia" featured in AIA's *Campus Report,* "Perhaps more cunningly than any other radical misfit group, they [homosexuals] have exploited our society's inherent tolerance. They have used our dislike of being called names or of being thought intolerant to intimidate and silence us."

Exactly the opposite is true. As recently as March 1996, conservative campus groups have stopped queer identity groups from attaining recognition as official campus organizations. Conservative disdain for the "homosexual lifestyle" has prompted groups like The Campus Crusade for Christ (CCC) to purchase ads in student dailies denouncing homosexuality. It is important to note that anti-Semitic organizations have purchased similarly intimidating ads denying the Holocaust in publications nationwide.

On October 3 and 4, 1995, just days before the annual celebrations for National Coming Out Day, testimonial ads appeared in The *Daily Star*, a Southwest Texas State University newspaper. The following are excerpts:

"I Know What It's Like to be Rejected by the Men I Should Have Been Able to Trust the Most"
by Anthony Falzarano, husband, father, former homosexual

I was lonely and isolated as a child. My father was psychologically absent, and my older brother would taunt me for being intelligent and not very athletic.... I was so desperate for male affirmation and touch that when a school teacher showed me attention, I was easy prey. I was sexually abused by at least four others by the time I hit 18.... [W]hen I went to college, there were those who were ready to help this broken kid accept a gay identity. And I bought it hook, line and sinker.... until a Christian man helped me see that I would never be satisfied in any life outside of God's purpose for me... So, don't buy the lie. You don't have to be gay.

"Being Lesbian Wasn't an Issue for Me. I Was Happy. But Then Someone Changed My Life Forever"
by Dawn Killion, former lesbian activist

...I'd been rejected by men, ridiculed all my life for being a tomboy.... As a lesbian, it was great to finally have an identity that fit. I loved being gay but down deep inside, I wondered if living like this was right. Of course, I didn't think there was any way out. I mean, I was born this way, right? So why did I feel the doubt? When I let Christ into my life,... I learned how He had a different purpose for my life and saw how His unconditional love helped me to heal the pain I'd covered for so long I really thought I belonged before, but believe me, there's no better life than being with God.

These "testimonies" promote anti-gay sentiments and the propagandized myth that child sexual molestation is commonly committed by gay men. Both ads end with the slogan "there is another way out" and are part of a project called "Every Student's Choice," a distortion of gay rights campaign rhetoric. They also portray homosexuality as a voluntary (and therefore reversible) choice that defies "God's natural law." Wielding such rhetoric, Exodus International (EI) and other groups are dedicated to "converting" homosexuals to heterosexuality.

Fighting anti-gay rhetoric on your campus can be tough, especially when many progressive organizations are not committed to advancing equality for gays, lesbians, bisexuals and transgendered people. However, effective tools for education and organizing are available from the National Gay and Lesbian Task Force Policy Institute at (202) 332-6483. You can also call the "Every Student's Choice" at 1-800-236-9238 to let them know what you think about their attempts to promote homophobia on college campuses.

Additional resources include the documentary film *One Nation Under God*, which exposes EI and their agenda, and *When Hate Groups Come to Town: A Handbook of Effective Community Responses*, 2nd Edition, 1992, published by the Center for Democratic Renewal.

Defunding the Left

by Rich Cowan and Jeremy Smith

Since the early 1990s, Right-wing think tanks and conservative youth organizations have made it a priority to eliminate student-fee funded activities, particularly for student organizations and publications which are concerned with human equality and environmental justice.

Terry Laban / In These Times

Nationwide campaigns have been launched against the U.S. Student Association (USSA) and Public Interest Research Groups (PIRGs), as well as against states and local groups.

The Eagle Forum Collegians (EFC), a Christian Right group headed by Phyllis Schlafly, has set up a project with the title "Defund USSA," which aims to cut the training and lobby group's funding from individual student governments. A 1995 article in *Eagle Eye*, the EFC newsletter,

describes the successful drive for the Northern Arizona University student government to withdraw its support from USSA, which they accuse of being "unaccepting of political ideologies not consistent with the leftward leaning thinking [sic]."

Meanwhile, the Center for the Study of Popular Culture (a.k.a. the Individual Rights Foundation) has filed a lawsuit against the Public Interest Research Groups (advocacy organizations that depend on student fees to function). Although the most recent attack is on Oregon

PIRG, branches in Massachusetts, New York, and New Jersey have had to fight to keep funding.

California was hard hit. A 1993 decision by the Supreme Court of California, *Smith v. Regents,* prohibited the use of compulsory student fees for funding political activities. Dozens of progressive student publications and organizations were defunded. Right-wing campus groups were not significantly affected by the ruling.

Naturally, the Republican House of Representatives has tried to get in on the act. In the summer of 1995, Rep. Ernest Istook (R-OK) introduced an amendment that would have denied federal funds to an institution of higher education where funds "derived from tuition, student activity fees or other charges... is used for the support of an organization that is engaged in lobbying or seeking to influence public policy." Due to grassroots student action and lobbying, the amendment was killed in committee; however, many observers are expecting a return of the "Campus Gag Rule."

What is the strategy behind defunding student organizations? Now that the campus far Right has built up such a large financial infrastructure, they do not need funding from student governments and activity fees. At Yale, outside funding provided to Right-wing groups exceeds all the funding provided to other groups through the student activities fee, according to *Newsweek* ("The Power of the Purse," May 15, 1995). With budgets in the hundreds of thousands of dollars, Right-wing student organizations simply do not need the support of the students that they supposedly represent. The effort to shift control of student political expression from the campus to outside corporate and religious institutions is clearly designed to change the balance of power on campus.

Ugly Law

by Michael Kennedy

In the pre-amble of the Virginia Bill for Establishing Religious Freedom, Thomas Jefferson wrote that "to compel a man to furnish contributions of money for the propagation of opinions which he disbelieves, is sinful and tyrannical." More than 200 years later, the case *Rosenberger v. Rector and Visitors of the University of Virginia* represents yet another example of how religious forces are continuing to impose their agenda upon the nation's public sector. As a result of this effort by the Christian Right to open up government institutions – namely education – to religion, the public has lost an important battle in the war for secular government.

In a five to four decision written by Justice Anthony M. Kennedy and concurred by Chief Justice Rehnquist and Justices O'Connor, Antonin Scalia, and Clarence Thomas on June 29, 1995, the Court concluded that the University of Virginia cannot deny funding to the appellant's Christian evangelical magazine *Wide Awake* under the Free Speech Clause of the First Amendment. The decision is fraught with logical inconsistencies, inaccurate categorizations of speech and viewpoint content, a clouding of issues regarding separation of church and state and a manipulation of the legal right to freedom of speech supported by the first amendment.

The issue began when Ron Rosenberger, then a student at University of Virginia (UVA), pursued reimbursement from the University Student Activities Fee (SAF) for approximately $5,900 in printing costs for Wide Awake. To understand the circumstances of this case, it is important to first briefly outline university policies concerning student organizations. For a student group to become eligible for SAF funding, it must first be recognized as a Contracted Independent Organization (CIO), a status available to any group with a student majority membership, officers that are full-time students, and that complies with UVA procedural requirements. CIO's are allowed access to UVA facilities including meeting rooms and computer terminals. Some CIO's are eligible to apply for funds from the Student Activities Fee (a result of a $14 mandatory charge per student per semester). Student activities which are excluded from SAF support include religious activities.

In its appeal before the Supreme Court, Rosenberger and his organization, Wide Awake Productions (WAP), maintained that the University had suppressed the dissemination of fundamentalist Christian views by denying them access to SAF funds. The Court affirmed that WAP had acquired CIO status soon after it was organized, and that "this is an important consideration in this case, for had it been a 'religious organization', WAP would not have been accorded CIO status." Judging by the guidelines submitted earlier concerning CIO's, however, there is no stipulation regarding the ideological nature of an "organization." The distinction was applied only when WAP tried to get SAF funds. Then the "religious organization" became "religious activity", which can be denied funds under UVA regulations. This is not to say, of course, that a religious organization must be inactive to be a CIO, but that in making such distinctions, the university accurately and correctly draws the line between protecting religious speech and not promoting religion.

One of the most profound inconsistencies on the part of the Court is the assertion that "there is no difference in logic or principle, and no difference of constitutional significance, between a school using its funds to operate a facility to which students have access, and a school paying a third-party contractor to operate the facility on its behalf." Therefore, whatever incidental costs arise to keep a meeting room well lit, or adequately heated, are equal in significance to a six thousand dollar reimbursement payment to cover the costs of printing a magazine which the university's official guidelines prohibit. This logic erases any authority that the university might have in determining the direction and use of its funds, and undermines any clear distinction between religious and non-religious material.

The Court's reasoning that payment to a "third-party contractor" does not sufficiently meet the criteria for the prohibited direct payment to religious activity is a farce. As Justice Souter writes in his dissent, this implies that "the State could simply hand out credit cards to religious institutions and honor the monthly statements."

Finally, in the precedent *School District of Grand Rapids v. Ball,* the Court held that "no tax in any amount, large or small, can be levied to support any religious activities or institutions, whatever they may be called, or whatever form they may adopt to teach or practice religion." In the *Rosenberger vs. Rector* decision, however, the Court maintains that the SAF is not a tax, but simply an "exaction upon the student."

The Court attempts to provide clear guidelines on the kind of speech that can be regulated by the University. On the one hand, the institution can restrict speech based on the content of that speech insofar as it is "acting to preserve the limits of the forum it has created." Therefore, the University has every right to restrict religious speech in the interest of church and state separation, or hate speech in the interest of the public well-being. On the other hand, the institution may not restrict speech based on the viewpoint of the person(s) involved.

In *Rosenberger vs. Rector,* the Court has decided that UVA had attempted the latter — discriminating against *Wide Awake* magazine because of the religious viewpoints of its editors — because the content of the magazine addresses "personal and community issues, especially those relevant to college students at UVA," among them "racism, crisis pregnancy, stress, and eating disorders." In properly responding to this assertion, however, Justice Souter contends that these "facially secular topics become platforms from which to call readers to fulfill the tenets of Christianity in their lives."

In reality, *Wide Awake's* content demonstrates how the magazine serves as a pulpit from which the evangelistic Rosenberger and his associates are attempting to bring their Christian mission to the masses and, in their own words, "to challenge Christians to live, in word and deed, according to the faith they proclaim and to consider what a personal relationship with Jesus Christ means." As the Court concluded in *School District of Grand Rapids v. Ball,* "although Establishment Clause jurisprudence is characterized by few absolutes, the Clause does absolutely prohibit government-financed or government-sponsored indoctrination into the beliefs of a particular religious faith."

Michael Greve, co-founder of the Center for Individual Rights, the public interest law firm that represents Rosenberger, claims that the argument that government does not subsidize religion is phony, noting that the government gives police and fire protection to churches. In so doing, Mr. Greve equates emergency protection from death and destruction with direct financial sponsorship and public support of a publication aimed at Christian religious conversion. The Center for Individual Rights, along with other Christian Right groups, is also responsible for bankrolling the case.

Barry W. Lynn, Executive Director of Americans United for Separation of Church and State, calls the Court's decision in *Rosenberger vs. Rector* "miserable... Evangelism should be supported by the voluntary donations of the faithful, not extracted forcibly from other Americans who don't share those beliefs." Lynn said anti-separationist groups are sure to try to build on this decision to further lower the wall between church and state, particularly through advocacy of "vouchers" for religious schools. He warned, "TV preacher Pat Robertson and his Religious Right allies are certain to use this decision as a stepping stone toward broad-based taxpayer support of religious schools and other institutions."

The Supreme Court ruled that the University of Virginia was engaging in viewpoint discrimination (which is illegal) rather than content discrimination (which is legal) in its decision to deny funding to *Wide Awake* magazine. The Court did so on the basis that the issues discussed in the magazine are purely secular, and it is only the viewpoint of the editors, not the magazine's text itself, that is Christian evangelical. The following are excerpts from the magazine:

Wide Awake on racism

God calls us to take the risks of voluntarily stepping out of our comfort zones and to take joy in the whole richness of our inheritance in the body of Christ. We must take the love we receive from God and share it with all peoples of the world. Racism is a disease of the heart, soul, and mind, and only when it is extirpated from the individual consciousness and replaced with the love and peace of God will true personal and communal healing begin.

Wide Awake on eating disorders

As thinking people who profess a belief in God, we must grasp firmly the truth, the reality of who we are because of Christ. Christ is the Bread of Life (John 6:35). Through Him, we are full. He alone can provide the ultimate source of spiritual fulfillment which permeates the emotional, psychological, and physical dimensions of our lives.

Wide Awake on their recent circumstances

We Christians can't, upon the denial of an appropriations check, cower back into our closets of anonymity, quiet and defeated, to rot forever. We have a story to tell. We have good news to share. And, check or no check, our vocation consists of doing so for as long as God enables us... Out of our mute closet we've come tumbling; here we are, to awake and to be awakened, unto the glory of God on high.

Turning Back the Clock on Affirmative Action:
University of California and Hopwood vs. Texas

by Nari Rhee and Sonya Huber

> ...the use of race in admissions for diversity in higher education contradicts, rather than furthers, the aims of equal protection. Diversity fosters, rather than minimizes, the use of race. It treats minorities as a group, rather than as individuals. It may further remedial purposes but, just as likely, may promote improper racial stereotypes, thus fueling racial hostility.
> - Judge Jerry E. Smith, Fifth Circuit Court of Appeals, Hopwood v. State of Texas.

Like an army marching in lockstep across the national political landscape, the assault on affirmative action policies — particularly in higher education — is gathering momentum state by state. Recent events in California and Texas bear tremendous symbolic and legal significance for the future of university policies that attempt to provide equitable access to women and students of color, or to foster gender and racial equity in hiring and promotion.

Corruption of Governance: the UC Regent Decision

In California, the initiative came from the Governor's office. Regent Ward Connerly, an African American appointed to the twenty-six member UC Board of Regents by Governor Pete Wilson, introduced resolutions SP-1 and SP-2 in Spring 1995. The two proposals attempted to ban the use of race and sex criteria in admissions and hiring, respectively. According to Connerly, a majority of Regents had assured him that they opposed any use of racial preferences. On July 20, over 1000 students converged at the UC San Francisco Laurel Heights campus to make their voices heard in favor of affirmative action, along with 100 elected officials, UC faculty, and community leaders, and 300 media representatives. Public comments were limited to an appalling 30 seconds per person.

Democratic process was, at most, symbolic, since most of the votes had been secured beforehand. Seventeen out of eighteen appointed seats had been filled by Republican governors, and Wilson himself had hand-picked seven. According to Irma Munoz of UC Student Association (UCSA), "Regents get appointed in reward for campaign contributions. Most of the recent appointees have donated over $200,000 to Wilson's campaign funds." At the end of the day, SP-1 and SP-2 narrowly passed.

UC Faculty Senate Votes in Favor of Rescinding SP-1 and SP-2			
Berkeley	124-2	Riverside	85-4
Davis	122-6	San Diego★	36-15
Irvine★	25-0	San Francisco	40-0
Los Angeles★	54-9	Santa Barbara★	35-1
		Santa Cruz	72-0

★ in the Representative Assembly; others in the entire Division
[Source: Aftermath #2, complied by Professor Charles Schwartz.]

In passing these resolutions, UC Board of Regents contradicted the will of the Chancellors and the majority of students and faculty at all nine UC campuses. In addition to intense lobbying by the UCSA and the various student assemblies, thousands of students vocalized their support for affirmative action at demonstrations on every campus, comprising as much as 20% of the student body on some campuses. The Faculty Committee to Rescind SP-1 and SP-2 collected 7000 signatures for a petition calling on the Regents to rescind their decision. Between October 1995 and January 1996, all nine UC Faculty senates echoed this demand. Despite this opposition, SP-1 and SP-2 were not revoked. Instead, the debate was soon intensified due to the introduction of Proposition 209 (the California Civil Rights Initiative), a referendum initiative to bar affirmative action in all state business.

Hopwood vs. State of Texas

The Fifth US Court of Appeals ruled that University of Texas law school admissions policies, which considered applicants in separate ethnic pools with different LSAT score criteria, violated the Fourteenth Amendment guarantee of equal protection under the law by giving preference to blacks and Hispanics over whites. The litigants were four white students, led by Cheryl Hopwood, who claimed that they had been denied admission to the UT Law School because of their race. Hopwood had put herself through school, was married to a military officer, and had a severely handicapped child.

Judge Jerry E. Smith concluded that her experiences would have been a contribution to the school, and that she had been discriminated against because her test scores would have qualified her for admission if she had been black or Hispanic.

The UT Law School defended its system on the basis of the 1978 University of California v. Bakke Supreme Court ruling that universities' "compelling interest" in diversity justified racial preferences. In addition, their target goals were rather modest: 10% Mexican-Americans and 5% blacks. However, the Fifth Circuit marshaled a much narrower definition of "compelling interest" as remedy for specific past wrongs. The UT Law School failed the "strict-scrutiny" test because it hadn't had an explicitly discriminatory policy against blacks in more than 30 years, and had never barred Mexican-Americans. Notably, all three Fifth Circuit judges were Reagan and Bush appointees.

The Fifth Circuit covers Texas, Louisiana, and Mississippi. UT appealed the case to the Supreme Court, which declined to hear the case in July 1996, on the basis that the UT Law School policy of considering applicants in separate pools was clearly illegal. The ruling signals a defeat for the principle of affirmative action, and could jeopardize diversity targets at US professional schools.

The Office of Civil Rights of the Department of Education has been considering whether to launch a formal investigation of UT; OCR has threatened to withhold $2 billion in education funding because UT may be violating The Texas Plan, and agreement to de-segregate reached by the OCR and the Texas state government in the early 1980s.

A group of students at the University of Texas organized the Committee on Post-Hopwood Political Strategies in Spring of 1997 to draw attention to the continued decrease in application. At the University of Texas, applications among African-American students have decreased 21%; Latino student applications are down 17%, and Native American applications are down 50%. UT's law school reported that it admitted only 10 African American students, down from 65 in 1996, and only 29 Latinos, down from 69 in 1996. Any financial aid that ethnic minority students receive is threatened until the legislature reaches a decision on whether any preference based on race is legal in Texas.

The Impact of SP-1 and SP-2

The effects of the UC Board of Regents folly are already being felt: systemwide applications from students of color have dropped by over 10%, according to the Student Affirmative Action/Equal Opportunity Program office at UC Santa Cruz. Furthermore, the implementation of

SP-1 and SP-2 will have a devastating impact on the admission, hiring, and promotion of women in math and science programs, many of which currently have severe problems of discrimination.

UC's new colorblind admissions policy has had immediate effects. In the spring of 1997, UC Law Schools reported a drastic decrease in the numbers of African American and Latino students accepted, and not all of these students will choose to attend these schools, making the final numbers even smaller. UCLA School of Law accepted only 21 African American applicants, down 80% from 1996. At UC Berkeley, Boalt Hall Law School accepted half the number of Latinos accepted in 1996. UC officials expect a similar pattern to emerge at UC's 600 other graduate schools this summer. The university's ban on considering race, ethnicity or gender in admissions will be extended to undergraduates in 1998.

A study by Linda Wightman of the University of North Carolina determined that of the 3,435 African-American applicants accepted to at least one law school in 1990-1991, only 20% would have been admitted on the basis of only grade point averages and LSAT scores. However, African-American students showed no significant differences in rates of graduation from law school or passing the bar. Thomas Kane, an economist at Harvard University's John F. Kennedy School of Government said the new method will not produce the same diversity, leaving African-Americans and Latinos badly underrepresented.

The political assault against affirmative action has gained momentum during a time of economic uncertainty, when higher education is increasingly necessary for survival in the labor market, and people — particularly the white working and "middle" classes — are anxious about "getting theirs."

The message is clear to the hundreds of thousands of students who get second-rate preparation for college because of institutionalized racism and sexism: They don't deserve higher education and the opportunity to overcome barriers they themselves had no hand in setting up. Their full participation in society is not a priority.

The Future of Affirmative Action

There are clear connections between the attack on support for affirmative action on campus and beyond the university. The Proposition 209 ballot question was co-authored by Ward Connerly, the Regent who helped to destroy affirmative action at UC, Proposition 209 was worded to sounded like it supported civil rights, when in fact it would eliminate affirmative action. Conservative supporters of the measure brought in $6.2 million, and outspent their opponents by a ratio of 2:1.

Paid petition circulators collected 1 million of the 1.2 million signatures, at a rate of up to $1 per signature.

On the side of affirmative action, Californians for Justice (CFJ, a statewide PAC) working in conjunction with community-based and labor organizations, geared up to get out the anti-209 vote in marginalized communities. The Feminist Majority organized a "Freedom Summer" to help register voters in areas with traditionally low voter turnout. During the campaign, the approval rating for Prop. 209 dropped from 75-80% to 54%, but ultimately it passed narrowly.

Legal action was taken immediately by the Coalition for Economic Opportunity, a broad-based coalition led by ACLU and including California Federation of Labor, NAACP, NOW, Asian-Indian Association of America, which had filed a lawsuit on November 6 to challenge the constitutionality of Prop 209. Despite a court ruling in November which delayed implementation, a federal appeals court upheld the legality of Prop. 209 in April of 1997. Majority judges based their ruling on the 14th Amendment, arguing that the U.S. aims to create a political system in which race no longer matters. They argue that affirmative action is not race blind and is therefore unfair. The majority decision, not coincidentally, was produced by two Reagan appointees and one judge appointed by Bush.

This decision opens the way for similar anti-affirmative action campaigns around the country. Proposition 209 co-author Ward Connerly has begun a new organization called the American Civil Rights Institute, which plans to launch similiar initiatives in states including Florida, Arizona, Colorado, Ohio, and Michigan. Tom Wood, a co-author of Proposition 209, is the executive director of the California Association of Scholars, a branch of the National Assocation of Scholars (NAS). The NAS is a conservative group of faculty and administrators that oppose multi-culturalism and may spearhead attacks to affirmative action in the form of ballot initiatives in other states.

A national poll found that though people may react negatively to the politically charged phrase "affirmative action," these same people say that they believe in measures to ensure ethnic and gender diversity in universities and workplaces. Grassroots mobilization and education, coalition building, and a carefully planned and executed strategy are key factors to successfully fighting heavily funded campaigns to turn back the clock on social justice.

Little Right Lies:
Anti-Affirmative Action Propaganda

By Nicole Newton, Rich Cowan, and Theo Emery

The Young America's Foundation (YAF) began distributing a brief on affirmative action to campus conservatives in the fall of 1995. A critical examination of its arguments offers some weapons against the rhetoric bandied by young conservatives in their assault against affirmative action policies.

Written by Matthew Schenk, a 1995 Swarthmore College graduate, the brief's entire argument is founded upon the following definition of affirmative action:

> Affirmative action, in all cases, is discrimination. Affirmative action seeks to advance members of 'underrepresented' groups by taking factors other than merit into account in the hiring and admissions process.

Manufactured to fit the Foundation's agenda, this is a blatantly inaccurate legal definition of affirmative action policy as it has evolved through decades of jurisprudence. Affirmative action is designed to make hiring and admissions more meritocratic by balancing out discriminatory tendencies in institutions and society at large.

Schenk uses affirmative action interchangeably with quotas, and argues that it results in mass hiring and admissions of unqualified persons. The 1978 Supreme Court case *Regents of the University of California v. Bakke*, found quota-based admissions illegal but legitimized consideration of a candidate's race as one factor among many.

Based on his definition of affirmative action, it's easy for Schenk to subvert the civil rights heritage for his own ends. He invokes Reverend Martin Luther King Jr.'s words from the 1963 March on Washington that "some day people will not be judged by the color of their skin but by the content of their character." Schenk then smugly accuses unnamed "civil rights activists" of making "color a divisive issue."

Affirmative action opponents try to deflect criticisms of being racist by invoking the support of token persons of color who have been propelled to prominence by conservative backing. The YAF brief quotes at length Dinesh D'Souza's controversial book *The End of Racism*. Schenk neglects to mention that the infamous book has been roundly condemned by scholars of all colors and political persuasions, and prompted the resignation of two prominent black conservatives, Robert L. Woodson and Glenn C. Loury, from the board of the American Enterprise Institute where D'Souza is in residence.

Schenck also identifies University of California Regent Ward Connerly, who spearheaded the UC affirmative action decision, as one of "increasing numbers of black leaders and intellectuals [who] have begun to seriously question the basic philosophical foundations of affirmative action." Mr. Schenk neglects to report that at least two of the four mentioned — Connerly and Supreme Court Justice Clarence Thomas — personally benefited from affirmative action, but in the corrupting glare of power, appear to have changed their minds.

Shelby Steele, author of *The Content of our Character*, is another black conservative who has taken a stand against affirmative action. The brief quotes:

> The concept of historic reparation grows out of man's need to impose a degree of justice on the world that does simply not exist.... Blacks cannot be repaid for the injustice done to the race, but we can be corrupted by society's guilty gestures of repayment.

But the notion of historic reparation does not form the basis of actual affirmative action policy, as Schenk implies through the use of this quote. Most policies address current realities of discrimination in society at large. Only when an institution is proven to have practiced blatant, systematic discrimination (such as a fire department deliberately excluding people of color in hiring) are aggressive measures such as quotas legally justified.

In a peculiar twist of logic, Schenk echoes the argument that affirmative action perpetuates what Steele calls the "myth of black inferiority." He states that black students are "bumped" up by affirmative action to institutions for which they are not prepared, causing dropout rates as high as 70%. However, a large body of scholarship on self-esteem — some of it by Shelby Steele's own brother — suggests that attrition results from internalization of years of social and institutional abuse directed at non-white communities. Schenk also seems deaf to the complaints of many working class students of color that they are isolated and alienated in institutions dominated by white, middle- and upper-class students and faculty. Schenk's claim that affirmative action causes high drop-out rates implies that these students are proportionately less intelligent, qualified, or motivated than whites.

The brief's final arguments against affirmative action are the most offensive. Schenk cites statistics from *U.S. News* that 91% of schools report self-segregation among black students. His conclusion: so why bother? He quotes University of South Carolina professor Steven Yates, who believes "preferential policies are a primary cause of the racial troubles haunting American college and university campuses." Taken to its logical conclusion, this suggests that resentful white students assail non-whites because of affirmative action, and not because of their own racism or threatened sense of entitlement.

Like almost all conservative arguments against affirmative action, most of the above arguments rest heavily on the myth of meritocracy. Meritocracy is the idea that in this system, the worthy will succeed; and by implication, those who

Terry Laban / In These Times

don't succeed must not be worthy. Ultimately, it is a rationalization for the status quo. As observed by Troy Duster, director of the Institute for the Study of Social Change and professor of sociology at UC Berkeley, "With privilege and power comes the unwitting, unthinking, reflexive arrogance that says it's normal." Such is the foundation of most conservative arguments against affirmative action: an irrational belief that the current racialized, gendered hierarchy is somehow normal.

Fooling the Public:
The Right and Student Aid

by Nova Ren Suma and Rich Cowan

Accepting recent Republican statements at face value, we would think student aid has always been a high priority in the minds of the Right. We would see this commitment demonstrated by increased funding for Pell Grants and work-study, by efforts to retain programs such as State Student Incentive Grants (SSIG), and above all by assurances that students and their families would pay the least amount of money with reduced hassle through Republican-backed student loan programs.

But the Republicans are wearing masks to fool the public. Some who now tout their support for higher education voted for the largest student aid cuts in history in 1995, and still support a reversal of reforms that have saved taxpayers and students billions of dollars.

How big is the student aid bill?

To help separate fact from fiction, here is some background information. About half of the 14.5 million students in the U.S. receive student aid. Almost 80% of the money these students receive is in the form of loans.

The student loan program mostly pays for itself. In FY 1997, which began in October 1996, students were expected to receive $33.7 billion in loans. Funding this program will cost taxpayers about $3 billion, most of which goes to cover the interest exemption students enjoy while still in college.[1]

The rest of the student aid budget, about $9 billion in FY 1997, comes directly from the treasury. About 10% of that is for work-study and the rest for grants, primarily Pell Grants. Student aid amounts to less than 1% of the federal budget and less than 10% of the deficit.[2]

In the mid-70s, Pell Grants provided 80% of the cost of the average public institution. Now they provide only 35%, according to US PIRG and the US Student Association.[3]

Opening Debate: the Contract With America

Reflecting an ideological stand against federal government involvement in education, Representatives Newt Gingrich and John Kasich targeted student aid programs in their plans to "balance the budget" by 2002. At the same time, they proposed a $245 billion tax cut for the wealthiest Americans. In February of 1995, Gingrich said that students should have to work for their Pell Grants, while Kasich proposed ending the interest exemption on student loans. In order to "balance the budget," Republican leaders claimed that they needed to cut $20 to $25 billion from higher education, again over the seven-year period from 1996-2002.

Needless to say, these proposals did not go over well on campus, with over 100 student demonstrations that spring against the "Contract On America." However, the Republican leadership pushed on with their plan. On August 4, 1995, the House of Representatives passed a budget that contained loan cuts of $10.2 billion over seven years[4] and cuts of $600 million in grants and fellowships in just one year.[5]

At the same time, the Republicans adopted a remarkable strategy: to claim that they done the opposite of what they had just done. On September 11th, the House Republican Conference released a memo stating, "GOP funds biggest Pell Grant Award," touting the fact that the House budget proposal would offer a maximum award of $2,400 to some Pell recipients. They conveniently failed to mention that their plan would reduce the total number of Pell recipients by 280,000 students, and total Pell funding by $482 million.[6]

Then, on September 28, College Republican National Committee (CRNC) Chairman Joe Galli sent a memo titled "Student Loans and Balancing the Budget" to campus chapters, stating that "Clinton and the Democrats" were creating "a student loan scare campaign in order to push his latest socialist policy down the throats of Americans."[7] This memorandum noted that "money available for student loans will increase 50% over the next seven years" under the Republican plan. The memo failed to note that the same increase in loan programs would be achieved in only 3 years under the Clinton plan, without any increase in the budget deficit.[8]

The lies continued. In November, the College Republicans distributed a posterboard sized sign on college campuses which said that Republicans would not "eliminate the six-month grace period for loan repayment" (even though they proposed charging interest during the "grace" period) and that their plan "Eliminates Clinton's Direct-Lending plan, saving $1.5 trillion over 7 years."[9] Apparently, they meant to say $1.5 billion because $1.5 trillion is larger than the combined tuition of all students in the U.S!

Second Deception: the 1997 Budget

The 1996 budget was finally approved in April of 1996 after a budget impasse shut the government down twice. It ended up striking most cuts in loan programs in favor of a $1.3 billion decrease in Pell Grants. Apparently, this did not go over well on the campaign trail. By September of 1996, when Congress was about to approve the 1997 budget, the Republican Congress joined the Democrats in a bidding war over student aid increases. The resulting increases in Perkins, SSIG, TRIO, Workstudy and Pell programs provided Republicans with some good news to bring back to their districts, but actually were a net decrease over FY 1995 levels. According to US PIRG's Higher Education Project Director Ivan Frishberg, these token increases "do nothing to account for increased tuition costs and other increases to the cost of living, and increased enrollments."

Direct Lending

Much of the debate in 1996 focused on the Clinton Administration's proposals to increase the number of schools participating in direct lending, a program developed by the Bush administration and Rep. Thomas E. Petri (R–WI). Direct lending provides federal loan money to colleges, bypassing banks and loan guaranty agencies. In its second year in 1995, the program constituted 40 percent of the total loan volume. Though created by Republicans, the program was viciously attacked by

Federal Funding for Student Aid Programs 1995-1997 (Millions of Dollars)

	1995	1996	1997
Pell Grant Program	6,200	4,900	5,900
Work Study Program	616	617	830
FSEOG	583	583	583
Perkins	158	93	158
SSIG	63	31	50
TRIO	463	463	500
Direct Loan Administration	n/a	436	491
Maximum Pell Grant Award ($)	2,340	2,470	2,700

Final Appropriations levels for fiscal year 1996-1997; Final spending levels for fiscal year 1995, *Source: United States Student Association and the American Council on Education* the new Republican Congress.

In December 1995, Congress voted to cap direct lending at 10 percent of total loan volume, but Clinton vetoed the measure. The following March, the House voted to freeze direct lending levels at 40 percent of total loan volume. Republicans dropped this proposal during the 1996 budget negotiations in April.

During the 1997 budget debate, in June, the House Appropriations Committee voted to rein in this program through severe cuts in the direct loan administration budget. According to the Washington Post, "Clinton officials, charging that Republicans are responding to political pressure from banks and loan guaranty agencies that profit from the $25 billion student loan industry, instead have been pushing to expand the program."[10]

Howard P. "Buck" McKeon (R-CA), Chairman of the House Subcommittee with jurisdiction over student aid programs, argued in late 1995 that money could be saved from higher education by "by requiring lenders and secondary markets to reduce their profit margin and by eliminating the government takeover of student lending." The Congressional budget office estimated in July 1996 that eliminating the direct student loan program would save taxpayers $1.5 billion over 7 years.

So which costs more: direct loans or private loans?

The Coalition for Student Loan Reform (CSLR), a national organization representing the banking industry, insists that direct loans do. Marie Clark, of the CSLR public affairs office claimed that the program would not actually save students the money they expected.[11]

However the US Student Association disagrees. According to Field Organizer Sandra England "Direct lending will save students and taxpayers money, as layers of bureaucracy are eliminated and billions of dollars in subsidies and special allowances are cut."

Proponents also argue direct lending saves money by eliminating banks' profits entirely. When Clark was asked if banks and guarantee agencies make a profit from student loans, she hedged, "Obviously banks make money off any money they loan. Guarantee agencies are given a certain amount of dollars for facilitating the process... but they are non-profit entities."

But according to the American Association of State Colleges and Universities (AASCU), many agencies do profit from the private lending system. An AASCU report titled "The Guarantee Agency Network: A System Designed for Waste and Abuse" pointed out that "Guarantee agencies are legislatively entitled to keep 27 percent of collections on defaulted loans; however, if the borrower does not default... the agency keeps nothing. This is a built-in, programmatic disincentive to prevent defaults."

In September 1996, Senator Paul Simon (D-IL) released a statement showing how the direct lending alternative had enabled the government to negotiate better deals with private banks administering existing student aid program. All tolled, "college students have about $1.9 billion more in their pockets today than if 1993 student loan reforms had not been enacted"[12] said Simon.

Republican Retreat

The campaign to cut student aid ended up a disaster for the Right. According to the PIRG's Frishberg, they "had to abandon a huge chunk of their agenda." As of this writing, the Clinton administration has proposed large increases in higher education funding, and the Republicans are again claiming to be on students' side by warning that a student aid funding boost will cause tuition increases. Note that the Right has not made similar statements about how increases in military spending might cause the price of weapons to increase. In fact, all Republican presidential candidates proposed eliminating the Department of Education.

Ideological opposition to social spending by the federal governent makes it hard to trust the Right as an ally in the struggle for educational access. And nowhere has the gulf between rhetoric and reality been greater than in the Right's posturing on the issue of student aid.

Notes

[1] White House Office of Management and Budget, *Budget of the U.S. Government,* F.Y. 1998 Tables, Office of Post Secondary Education, page 428. Enrollment estimate is from *Chronicle of Higher Education,* September 2, 1996.

[2] In FY 1996 the total U.S. budget was $1.56 trillion; the deficit was around $107.3 billion, *Budget of the U.S. Government,* page 303.

[3] Letter from Ivan Frishberg and Kazim Ali to Senator Arlen Specter, Sept. 9, 1996.

[4] Butts, Thomas, "Republican Budget: Impact on Education," memo quoting Congressional Budget Office numbers.

[5] "1996 Appropriations for the Education Department," *Chronicle of Higher Education,* August 18, 1995, p. A28.

[6] "The Big Lie about The Big Lie on Campus," in *The Chopping Block,* bulletin of the College Democrats of America, Friday, September 22, 1995.

[7] Galli, Joe, "Student Loans and Balancing the Budget" memo from College Republican National Committee, September 28, 1995.

[8] "Debate Heates Up over Expansion Plan for Direct Loan Program," *Chronicle of Higher Education,* February 24, 1995, p. A32.

[9] as quoted in e-mail message from Maureen McRae, Associate Dean, Office of Financial Aid, Glendale Community College.

[10] *The Washington Post,* July 2, 96.

[11] Telephone conversation with Marie Clark by Nova Ren Suma.

[12] Press Release from Sen. Paul Simon, September 12, 1996.

CONSERVATIVE CAMPUS ACTIVISM:

WHO ARE THE PLAYERS?

Dinesh D'Souza, photo illustration by Ben Leon

Snapshot of the Campus Right

Funding of 13 Key Groups, 1994-5 ($000)

Rank	Organization	Income	From Fdn. Grants
1	Intercollegiate Studies Institute	4,747	2,262
2	Center for the Study of Popular Culture	3,002	2,033
3	Federalist Society	1,237	809
4	National Association of Scholars	890	750
5	National Alumni Forum	663	240
6	Young Americas Foundation	3,658	228
7	Accuracy in Media★★	1,525	193
8	Leadership Institute	4,717	180
9	Education and Research Institute	340	168
10	Third Millennium	163	35
11	Eagle Forum Legal Defense & Education★★	1,003	30
12	Collegians Activated to Liberate Life	N/A	0
13	College Republican National Committee★	N/A	0
	Total of Grants Listed	**$21,945**	**$6,926**

Top 10 Funders of these Groups in 1994-5 ($000)

Rank	Foundation	$$ to 13 Groups	% of Total Giving
1	Sarah Scaife	1,825	16.1%
2	Lynde and Harry Bradley	1,106	4.6%
3	John M. Olin	870	5.4%
4	Henry Salvatori	455	23.3%
5	Allegheny	375	18.0%
6	Carthage	195	2.8%
7	William H. Donner	335	14.2%
8	Scaife Family	325	6.1%
9	Smith Richardson	205	2.0%
10	Castle Rock	225	10.1%

Methodology: Grant data is from the 4th Edition of Who Gets Grants, Who Gives Grants (1997) covering 800 large foundations from 1994-5. All groups received additional funds from individuals as well as from smaller foundations. Intercollegiate Studies Institute totals include the Madison Center for Educational Affairs, which merged with ISI in 1995. Total income data is from The Right Guide, 3rd Edition (1997) and Third Millenium budget documents.

★The College Republicans, as a partisan organization, do not receive any foundation grants.

★★Funding received by a parent group; some may be for campus wing (Eagle Forum Collegians, Accuracy in Academia)

[Compiled by Harley Gambill and Rich Cowan, June 1997.]

13 Campus Right-wing Groups to Watch Out For

compiled by the CCO staff

Dozens of national right-wing groups operate on college campuses today (see Appendix E). The CCO staff has selected 13 groups that we feel have the greatest influence today. Membership figures were supplied by the organizations themselves, so their accuracy may vary. Here are descriptions of these groups:

Accuracy in Academia (AIA), a subsidiary of Reed Irvine's Accuracy in Media, caters to the "hard core" of student conservatism. AIA was established in Washington D.C. in 1985, and claims membership in excess of 200,000 on 1,500 campuses. Although these figures are obviously inflated, they may accurately reflect the distribution of AIA's *Campus Report*. This monthly newspaper is sent in bundles to AIA affiliated students and professors, who monitors incursions by the "liberal left" into the university. AIA also provides an annual conference for its active membership.

AIA frequently bashes homosexuality in order to appeal to its base of individual donors. In 1994 *Campus Report* printed an article defending campus gaybashers entitled "Hooray for Homophobia" — next to an article printing the home addresses of several members of the gay, lesbian, and bisexual student caucus of the U.S. Student Association.

According to the article's author, past executive director Mark Draper, AIA is dedicated to helping students keep "liberalism" out of the classroom. The group's information-gathering is done by affiliated students who keep tabs on professors, record statements, and collect syllabi and course descriptions. AIA estimates that 85% of American professors are "tenured liberals."

Draper states that AIA organizes campuses by recruiting students with solid grade point averages, who are willing "to seek out the little Stalinists in the faculty." AIA was roundly criticized in the mid-1980s by liberal academics including the president of MIT, for tactics which created a "chilling effect" on academic freedom.

Center for the Study of Popular Culture (CSPC) and Individual Rights Foundation (IRF) are dedicated to using the countercultural methods of the 60's to fight for Right-wing values in the 1990's.

Founded in 1989 by ex-hippie radicals David Horowitz and Peter Collier in 1989, the L.A.-based CSPC publishes an irreverent anti-PC monthly called *Heterodoxy*, which was distributed for free to hundreds of thousands of conservative and liberal faculty members in 1992-4. CSPC, which uses its proximity to Hollywood to critique the media, has campaigned against the Corporation for Public Broadcasting (PBS). The group stands up to feminists and fervently attacks liberals, as some 60s radicals did. They publish a pamphlet attacking affirmative action policies entitled "Liberal Racism." As a propaganda machine to divide the left, they received over $2 million in 1994-5 from foundations, in addition to donations from over 25,000 members.

In 1993, the CSPC founded the Individual Rights Foundation to focus "on cultural issues with emphasis on opposing ideological orthodoxies on college and university campuses across the country." IRF works with fraternity councils on campus, and litigates First Amendment lawsuits against hate speech codes. They have recently begun to attack the National Education Association and the California Teachers Association for their use of union dues to oust anti-labor incumbents from Washington.

The College Republican National Committee (CRNC), the college component of the Republican National Committee (RNC), was formed in 1892 at the University of Michigan. The College Republican agenda is to elect Republicans to seats at every level of government and attempt to defeat the "organized left" on their campus. The RNC provides campus chapters with materials, speakers, and "Fieldman Schools" where young conservatives are trained. In 1994 there were an estimated 1,100 college chapters with approximately 100,000 members.

CRNC chapters advocate defunding organizations like the US Public Interest Research Groups and the United States Student Association (USSA). The CR's were headed in 1984 by Ralph Reed, recent chair of the Christian Coalition. During Reed's tenure, the CR's used "stealth tactics" to take over dozens of progressive student governments.

In 1994, CRNC national headquarters in D.C. were shut down by the Republican Party for going too far right. Among other things, CRNC published articles announcing the formation of militia groups and advocating the formation of a third party in its national newsletter, *The Broadside*. The D.C. office was returned to CRNC in 1995, but their strength has decreased. The CRNC's big issue in 1995 was attacking student aid programs, hardly a membership builder. College Republicans were most active in 1996 at the local level, providing support to Republican candidates.

Collegians Activated to Liberate Life (CALL): CALL is an anti-choice organization based in Madison, WI. It boasts a presence on over 100 campuses. Founded in 1991 by Peter Hees, the group seeks to "create a Christian network among campus leaders... to increase and solidify their commitment to our Lord and His Children" and to "make abortion unthinkable." From face-to-face harassment to criminal destruction, CALL uses Operation Rescue-style tactics to invade women's health clinics and disrupt the lives of women seeking help. CALL is staffed by Christian students who usually take time off from school to work in the national office, coordinating CALL weekends, training students in civil disobedience tactics, and publishing a red, white and blue newsletter called *The Trumpet*.

Eagle Forum Collegians (EFC): Launched by Eagle Forum president Phyllis Schlafly in 1993, EFC is aimed at bringing the Forum's anti-feminist, militarist message to college campuses. Funded almost entirely by the nonprofit Eagle Forum Education and Legal Defense Fund, based in Elton, Illinois, EFC publishes a quarterly newsletter which they claim reaches 80,000 subscribers. The Eagle Forum's annual Leadership Summits, timed to coincide with the annual convention of the College Democrats, are attended mostly by conservative students interning on Capitol Hill each June. EFC's mission statement is "To provide students with the tools necessary to combat PC and liberalism on college campuses; and to educate and inform the public on relevant issues." The Eagle Forum claims credit for defunding the US Student Association at the University of Iowa.

Federalist Society (FS): Founded in 1982, the Federalist Society seeks to win over the next generation of lawyers and reorder "the legal system to place a premium on individual liberty, traditional values, and the rule of law," according to its brochure. The D.C.-based group has become a highly influential organization within the legal-political system with an annual budget of $700K, 10,000 members, and chapters at roughly 120 law schools. Since its inception, the organization has received hundreds of thousands of dollars from conservative foundations — Institute for Educational Affairs, Olin, Bradley, Scaife, and Smith Richardson.

Although the Society markets itself as a beleaguered conservative minority, they receive considerable support from judges in positions of power, including Supreme Court Justices Scalia and O'Connor, Chief Justice Rehnquist and federal judges Robert Bork and Alex Kozinski. Because of these ties, some law students actually join the Society as a career move.

Intercollegiate Studies Institute (ISI): Recently relocated to a 23-acre mansion in Delaware, ISI is the oldest and largest conservative campus group. It was founded by William F. Buckley, then an assistant to Senator Joseph McCarthy, in 1954. According to *Newsweek*, their 1995 budget was $3.5 million. ISI has a membership of 50,000, including 2,500 student and faculty representatives.

ISI's *Campus* is a student-run conservative magazine claiming distribution on 1,200 campuses. A glossy and professional-looking journal, *Campus* has regular features from conservative students across the country, and runs articles denouncing feminism, affirmative action, multiculturalism and anything progressive. The they say they work to promote the American ideal of "ordered liberty." One of the advisors to *Campus,* Jonathan Karl, recently used his journalism experience to become a network correspondent on Cable News Network.

In 1995, ISI absorbed the Madison Center for Educational Affairs' "Collegiate Network," a consortium of conservative magazines and newspapers operating on some of the nation's premier campuses, including the seven Ivy League Schools, MIT, Stanford, Georgetown, and Berkeley. This transition evidently reduced the size of the Collegiate Network, which had 72 member publications in the spring of 1994, and reached a low of 39 papers before rebuilding to 55 in late 1996.

According to Tanya Daley, former Program Officer and a 1992 graduate of Tufts University, the Collegiate Network started when students in Chicago were unhappy with student news coverage on their campus. Daley claimed that MCEA had the support of "a large proportion of Rhodes Scholars."

The Dartmouth Review is the one of the oldest and most prominent members of the Collegiate Network. Conservative think-tank author Dinesh D'Souza was one of its first editors. Former staff member Ben Strauss noted, "after college I am sure there are opportunities out there in organizations, think-tanks and radio shows." That was the case for D'Souza, who has toured the political talk-show circuit after receiving immense outside funding from conservative think tanks for his most recent book *The End of Racism.*

The Leadership Institute (LI): Founded during the Reagan administration and directed by Morton Blackwell, former domestic policy advisor to Ronald Reagan, LI offers a variety of programs to young conservatives. The Leadership Institute School hosts about 50 two-day classes each year on leadership identification and training, group organization, canvassing, voter registration, and the internet. LI's Capitol Hill Training School aims to prepare young conservatives to work successfully in Congress. The Student Publications School conducts annual training seminars for conservative campus journalists to correct what Mr. Blackwell calls the "tremendous liberal bias in news reporting and interpretation." According to their web site, "over 700 students have attended the student publications school in recent years. LI is responsible for training staff members on over 60% of conservative campus newspapers." The Institute also provides funding and support services to student newspapers. According to Blackwell, the directors, staff and graduates of the Institute are constantly "talent scouting" for conservative groups.

National Alumni Forum (NAF): A Right Wing alumni organization, NAF was founded by former Chair of the National Endowment for the Humanities Lynne Cheney in 1995. The organization claims in its mission statement that they are working to preserve and foster "free academic debate and the pursuit of truth." This translates into mobilizing conservative alumni to harass progressive administrators and faculty, opposing multicultural curricula, and leverage donations to their *alma mater* to effect Right-wing changes to university hiring and policy. The NAF has been very active in the Washington, DC area, attempting to discredit the administration of Trinity College and holding a press conference to accuse the English Department at Georgetown of anti-Shakespeare bias. The NAF publishes a newsletter called *Academe.*

National Association of Scholars (NAS): Founded at Princeton in 1988, NAS is an organization of state affiliates made up of faculty, administrators, and current grad students "committed to rational discourse as the foundation of academic life in a free society....reason, democracy and an open intellectual life." They are against affirmative action, multiculturalism and "political correctness." They support ethnic studies as long as it doesn't attack western institutions. They believe that other cultures' adaptations of Western ideas are a "striking testament to the universality of the values they embody." Western culture has absorbed aspects of other cultures, so therefore they are already represented.

NAS has over 40 affiliates, such as the Massachusetts Association of Scholars and California Association of Scholars. The New Mexico chapter recently wrote a letter to the president of Arizona State University, decrying the presence of Women's Studies, Chicago Studies, Minority Student Services, etc. as the "balkanization" of the campus.

NAS publishes a quarterly newsletter, *NAS Update*, and the journal *Academic Questions.* They provide research fellowships, faculty and executive search assistance, and a research center, and a speaker's bureau featuring such luminaries as antifeminist Christina Hoff Sommers.

The Education and Research Institute (ERI) National Journalism Center: Based in Washington, D.C., ERI's mission is "Education of Youth in Journalism." ERI was founded in 1977 and its "National Journalism Center" project are brainchildren of the American Conservative Union, a long-standing organization representing U.S. conservatives. Like the Leadership Institute, ERI provides job placement and journalism training for young conservatives. ERI publishes the *ERI Report;* it's annual budget totaled $420,000 in 1994. Examples of alumni supporters include these media and public relations moguls: Geoff Baum of C-SPAN, John Fund of *The Wall Street Journal,* Jody Hassett of CNN, Bill McGurn of *The Far Eastern Economic Review,* and Lisa Schiffren, a former speechwriter for Dan Quayle.

Third Millennium (3M): Originally billed as a "post-partisan" group of twenty-somethings working to cut the deficit, 3M was formed to represent "generation X" from a conservative economic perspective. Their founding treatise was ratified at a March 1993 meeting attended by four women and sixteen men, at the home of Ethel Kennedy. Shying away from "divisive issues" such as abortion, the death penalty, and sexism, Third Millennium's most pressing issue is "reform" of the Social Security system.

Though the group's deficit-busting politics are modeled on Lead or Leave and the Concord Coalition, they are more dangerous because its literature fosters a grassroots bipartisan image; the right-wing connections are covert. The group was founded by Jonathan Karl and Robert Lukefahr, both of whom served on the advisory board of *Campus,* the newspaper of the Intercollegiate Studies Institute. Almost half its founding members were affiliated with the Madison Center for Educational Affairs. They received funding from the Right-wing JM foundation in 1994, according to the foundation's annual report.

More recently, in line its pro-privatization stance, 3M has received funding from the insurance and financial services industries. According to a fiscal 1997 "donor list" published by Third Millennium, the group received funding from the foundations of AT&T, The Prudential, The Pinkerton Foundation, the JM Kaplan Fund, and received commitments of $190,000 for the period from July 1996 to January 1997.

Young America's Foundation, created in 1969 by a pro-war Vietnam Vet, is an offshoot of **Young Americans for Freedom (YAF).** Despite the similar name, the Virginia-based Foundation is entirely separate from YAF, which still exists but is overshadowed in influence by the Foundation. The Foundation boasts 7,000-members and the support of Newt Gingrich and Oliver North, who speak regularly at events for young conservatives. The Foundation's biggest event is its Annual Conservative Student Conference, attended recently by 400 young conservatives, who each paid $250 to attend.

During the Gulf War, the Foundation organized rallies in support of military intervention. More recently, they have focused on ending affirmative action policies nationwide. Charging that the liberal political agenda is destroying college campuses, they regularly launch attacks on liberal professors and student groups.

YAF offers conservative students a speaker's bureau which dispatches well-known conservative lecturers like Ronald Reagan, Phyllis Schafly, Dinesh D'Souza, G. Gordon Liddy, Barry Goldwater, and George Will.

YAF received a financial boost from the Reagan administration in 1982-3 consisting of over $110,000 in grants from the US Information Agency (see Appendix H).

OTHER RIGHT-WING GROUPS TO WATCH OUT FOR

Peter Hannan/ In These Times

The Center for Individual Rights (CIR) is a DC-based pro-bono, Right-wing law firm founded in 1989 by Michael Greve and lawyer Michael McDonald, both from the conservative Washington Legal Foundation. CIR received start up grants from the conservative Smith Richardson, Carthage, Bradley and John M. Olin foundations. The Center also received $30,000 from the Pioneer fund, a group that supports studies of supposed genetic differences between blacks and whites. According to McDonald, the firm has "built its name primarily in the fight against political correctness." CIR litigates against speech codes, sexual harassment codes, and affirmative action. Their most notorious cases are *Rosenberger v. UVA*, in which a former student challenged the university's refusal to fund a Christian newspaper, the *Hopwood v. UT Law School* reverse discrimination suit, and the James Maas case, which involves a Cornell professor's appeal of university findings that he sexually harassed four female students. Robert Detlefsen, the center's research director, maintains that many of their clients are "white male college professors because these are the folks who find themselves victimized by political correctness."

The Heritage Foundation (HF): Unquestionably the most influential Right-wing think-tank of the 1990's, HF started in 1973 with a $25,000 grant from the Coors Foundation. By 1984, HF staff totaled over 100 with an annual budget over $10 million. HF's staff and budget increased greatly during Reagan's second term.

HF does not rely on seasoned conservatives; it mainly employs recent conservative college graduates. It grooms young conservatives like former *Dartmouth Review* Editor's Dinesh D'Souza and Ben Hart. Prominent supporters to HF include Paul Weyrich of the Committee for the Survival of a Free Congress and Howard Phillips of the Conservative Caucus. The Heritage Foundation provides elite opportunities for aspiring young conservatives.

Students for America (SFA): SFA, located in Raleigh, North Carolina, is dedicated to advancing conservatism, patriotism and Judeo-Christian values. SFA claims 6,000 members on 175 campuses. According to SFA's statement of purpose, they are "the mirror image of the liberal student activists in the sixties."

Former Executive Director Jonathan Roberts claimed, "with the College Democrats and Republicans, party politics get in the way of issues." He encouraged students to opt for careers in professions like medicine, engineering, or academia and to "get out of the closet, into professions that liberals have capitalized on in the news media."

Ivy Leaguers for Freedom /Women for Freedom: Based in Dallas, Texas, Ivy Leaguers for Freedom is the brainchild of Wellesley College graduate Larissa Yanov, who first established Women for Freedom at her *alma mater*. The organization is dedicated to upholding the elite and exclusive nature of the Ivys and their "seven sister" schools. While decrying "political correctness," Ivy Leaguers has ironically suffered from Yanov's attempts to control the politics of local chapters, according to a 1995 article in the *Boston Globe*.

[This article incorporates reporting by Martin Boer, James Kilcoyne, Dalya Massachi, and Pamela Wilson.]

FROM CRADLE TO GRAVE:

THE RIGHT'S YOUTH TRAINING AND ALUMNI NETWORKS

Peter Hannan/ In These Times

Youth Training and the Strategy of the Right

by Rich Cowan

Buoyed by the Republican victory in Congress, young conservative organizers gathered in July 1995 at George Washington University to celebrate at the National Conservative Student Conference. "The revolution is about you," enthused keynote speaker Newt Gingrich to a cheering crowd of over 300. These students attended workshops and nightly dinner banquets where they met peers sharing similar views and mingled with conservative luminaries, including Ralph Reed, Oliver North, Jack Kemp, Dinesh D'Souza, and Sonny Bono. The Young Americas Foundation heavily subsidized the $1,000-per-person cost of this event.

This event demonstrated the high priority the Right gives to young activists. The success of the 17th annual National Conservative Student Conference was the culmination of a long-term investment in conservative student organizing which began even before the election of Ronald Reagan. A chief architect of this strategy was Reagan advisor Morton Blackwell, who wrote in *Conservative Digest* (1/85):

> Success in the political process is very largely determined by the number and effectiveness of the respective sides. After 25 years... I have learned that while it's possible to take a competent opportunist and make that person philosophically sound, it's far easier to take people who are committed philosophically and make them technically proficient... We are convinced that the conservative movement will increase its success in direct proportion to the number of new activists we create.

Blackwell's deeds followed his words. He founded the Virginia-based Leadership Institute in 1986, which has since provided free training on basic journalism and organizing skills to over 10,000 young conservatives. As Executive Director of the Council for National Policy (whose 400+ members include Reed, Richard Viguerie, Howard Phillips, Ed Meese, Pierre DuPont, and Pat Robertson), he formed a Youth Council of 84 young people who now participate in the council's annual strategy retreat.

When I was a student activist at MIT in the mid-1980s, our counterparts on the Right received political training. I now realize that its purpose was not only to counter our anti-apartheid and anti-SDI activism. The larger motive was to groom young people for future leadership positions. Ralph Reed's "stealth tactics" did not start with his Christian Coalition efforts to take over school boards; they started years earlier with College Republicans President Ralph Reed's campaign to take over liberal student governments.

The Opportunity for Tomorrow

We are fortunate today that as soon as the Right gained power in Congress, they ended their stealth tactics and revealed their agenda. The outcry against the budget cuts of the "Contract on America" restored a much-needed sense of unity and camraderie among progressive organizers, especially on college campuses. It defeated the Istook proposals to restrict student and nonprofit political activity. It bought us some time to increase our capacity to develop new organizers, in an environment where religious and economic conservative groups continue to invest at least $20 million annually for this purpose.

The silver lining in the black cloud of the "Republican Revolution" is that progressive politics — which only two years ago were stigmatized as "politically correct" — are respectable again. This year, the AFL-CIO's 1996 "Union Summer" campaign further popularized progressive politics on campus by providing paid training to 1,000 young activists. Many students who formed campus coalitions in 1995 are now forging linkages with community groups. Attacks on the social safety net and affirmative action have narrowed the gulf between community service and political action groups, and increased the involvement of students of color and low income students.

This increased participation can last beyond the 1996 election, if progressive organizations and foundations can take a cue from the Right, and develop a comprehensive and coordinated strategy to foster long-term political commitment among young high school and college activists. Here is the Right's strategy:

- Funding for youth activism and journalism is an investment to sustain the life of a movement. It develops future members and organizers and affects the intellectual discourse on campus — even though it may not quickly lead to electoral involvement or measurable policy changes at the national level.

- Grassroots training programs can be developed as long-term institutions serving and sustaining many groups, so that they will be less vulnerable to the funding fluctuations and shifting priorities of parent or single-issue groups.

- Students on different campuses need opportunities to come together regionally or nationally to develop the sense of participation in a national movement.

- Administrative and fundraising skills for maintaining membership organizations can be introduced to students while still in school. This can help campus organizations sustain themselves after individual members graduate and equip students to contribute to the stability of grassroots non-profit groups after they graduate.

- Paid internships, apprenticeships, and entry-level jobs that provide liveable wages can develop young talent and commitment, reducing burnout.

- Students need opportunities to interact with professors and organizer/ mentors who have been successful at maintaining their commitment to activism or journalism.

- Youth training, electoral efforts and community groups can be linked so that the energy expended to train a volunteer base for a political campaign can be used between elections, and so that electoral campaigns do not have to start from scratch.

- "Activism" is an ordinary part of democratic participation — not just for "policy wonks" or those on the ideological fringe.

Greater civic participation is needed to counter the antidemocratic trends toward corporate financing of the media and the exploitation by religious conservatives of low voter turnout. The linkage of thousands of student groups to community and labor groups can increase political fervent both on and off campus. The democracy movement of the 21st Century will increase its success in direct proportion to the number of new activists we can sustain.

Fear And Loathing at The Eagle Forum's 1995 Annual Leadership Summit

by Michael Kennedy

Phyllis Schlafly received notoriety for her staunch opposition to the Equal Rights Amendment, but her conservative activism didn't stop there. Founder of the Eagle Forum and President since 1972, her agenda has included the following: strengthening U.S. national defense, supporting the presidential nomination of Barry Goldwater, fighting abortion rights, and opposing the gay rights movement. She has authored several books, including *A Choice Not an Echo, The Gravediggers*, and *What's Wrong With Equal Rights for Women.*

In 1993, the Eagle Forum decided it was time to bring its message to college campuses. Schlafly warned conservatives that "liberals envision schools as the means to absolute equality, to 'political correctness,' and the eradication of religion." To quash progressive forces in colleges and universities, Schlafly launched the Eagle Forum Collegians (EFC), a network of campus affiliates actively opposed to "political correctness," multiculturalism, and women's and gay studies. Funded almost entirely by the nonprofit Eagle Forum Education and Legal Defense Fund, EFC publishes a quarterly newsletter, *The Eagle Eye,* and sponsors member con-

Phyllis Schlafly

ferences, or Leadership Summits. EFC's mission is "To provide students with the tools necessary to combat PC and liberalism on college campuses; and to educate and inform the public on relevant issues." (EFC Mission Statement). With 80,000 newsletter subscribers alone, the organization has become a conservative force on college campuses.

I attended the Eagle Forum Collegians' Second Annual Leadership Summit on June 22-23, 1995 in Washington, DC. Speakers at the summit included Congressman Duncan Hunter, Senator and Presidential nominee Phil Gramm, Senator James Inhofe, Congresswoman Helen Chenoweth, Senator Spencer Abraham, and others on issues ranging from immigration and national security to feminism and "freedom".

A doomsday address by Frank Gaffney, Jr. from the Coalition to Defend America, titled "Why Can't We Shoot Down Enemy Missiles?" provided an opening day highlight. He identified the single most important national security problem today as the situation portrayed in the film Crimson Tide. Mr. Gaffney described several world leaders as "zealots" and "delusional fruit cakes" designing strategic plans to do away with large pieces of the United States — maybe even your hometown! He blamed the 1972 Anti-Ballistic Missile Treaty for allowing a Crimson Tide scenario, and the federal government for instituting policy that allows "our people to remain vulnerable."

The first day concluded with an ice cream social in which participants listened to the Rush Limbaugh radio program.

The second day of the Leadership Summit focused on college campus politics. C-SPAN recorded the proceedings, including all thirty or so remaining student attendees. Phyllis Schlafly began with a presentation titled "Don't Fall For Feminist Follies." According to Schlafly, Simone DeBeauvoir was the "big mama of feminism," Betty Friedan is "a housewife that sat around feeling sorry for herself," US Supreme Court Justice Ruth Bader Ginsburg is a "bizarre... kooky... off the wall... anti-homemaker... radical feminist," and Anita Hill too is a "kooky... bizarre... radical feminist." "The feminist movement," she proclaimed, "is not compatible with common sense, with human nature."

Later, two former students who had led successful campaigns to defund the Public Interest Research Groups and the US Students Association on their respective campuses offered attendees advice on how to mount similar efforts. One tip was to attend "the Morton Blackwell Leadership Institute."

Pat Collins, the Yale University student publisher of *Light and Truth* responsible for inflammatory and inaccurate coverage of an affair involving the return of a $20 million gift to Texas oil billionaire Lee Bass, gave a presentation titled "Building Conservative Newspapers." His enlightened analysis: "liberals are just wrong, so what are they going to do?"

Ron Rosenberger, Program Officer at the Young America's Foundation, spoke about his victory as the plaintiff of the US Supreme Court case against the University of Virginia. This litigation resulted in a national precedent prohibiting the denial of public university funding for religious publications such as his Christian evangelical magazine *Wide Awake*. His speech was broadcast over C-SPAN.

After several more presentations, Phyllis Schlafly wrapped up the Leadership Summit with a farewell and praised the Eagle Forum Collegians as the "traditional voices for a new generation."

Conservatives Teach the Young

by the National Student News Service

Dozens of students from around the nation developed their political skills at the eighth annual Conservative Leadership Conference (CLC) held in November 1996 in Washington D.C. by the right wing Leadership Institute.

About half of the 275 CLC attendees were students, according to Leadership Institute President Morton Blackwell. Participants attended workshops on such topics as conservative organizing, campaigning, fundraising and activism.

Georgetown University junior Jeremy Brown said he was interested in many of the famous conservatives who spoke at the conference, including Presidential candidates Alan Keyes and Steve Forbes, Phyllis Schlafly of the Eagle Forum, and Oliver North of the Iran-Contra scandal. Brown asserted that the conservative movement on campus is "getting stronger, but is not yet strong." He added that he was very pleased with the outcome of the recent election.

"The way I see it, we've got a Republican Congress and a Republican President," Brown said.

Camille Remmert is an intern at the Leadership Institute who co-founded the College Republicans chapter at her school, York College of Pennsylvania. Remmert was attracted to the CLC after working for the pro-life movement on campus. A 20-year-old college junior, Remmert said people at the conference were "woven together over social concerns" such as fighting abortion and working for "a return to family values."

Remmert advised conservative students to develop their activism skills. "In general, I think conservatives need to learn more about political technology," she said. "You can't promote a belief unless you're willing to learn how to talk about it." Brown said fellow conservative students at Georgetown are working to "take on liberal professors and bring conservative speakers to campus." He added that the College Republicans and College Democrats play regular softball games at his school.

CLC workshop facilitators included Tom Atwood of the Heritage

Foundation, Chuck Cunningham of the Christian Coalition, Kris Ardzonne of the Eagle Forum, and Stan Ridgley of the Intercollegiate Studies Institute.

From a Leadership Institute recruitment flyer:

Feeling censored on your campus?

Want to have your views heard?

Learn how to start your own conservative campus publication.

Our two-day Student Publications School will give you the training you need.

The Leadership Institute will help you learn how to:

Gain donor and foundation support.

Start your own independent, conservative campus newspaper.

The Leadership Institute's Student Publications School teaches you the nuts and bolts of how to start and fund a paper or improve an existing one. Learn from expert faculty, including some of the best conservative fund-raisers and journalists in the country.

You can beat speech codes, multiculturalism and political correctness! Challenge the liberal campus news monopoly. Over 700 students have attended the Student Publications School in recent years. LI is responsible for training staff members on over 60% of conservative campus newspapers.

Keeping a Watch on Your School's Alumni

by Dalya Massachi, Michael Kennedy and Nicole Newton

Over the past several years, the Right Wing has become dissatisfied with simply funding campus organizations and guiding the new generation of young ultraconservatives. Conservatives have discovered a new source of support in conservative alumni. After swallowing propagandized information about "what's really happening" at their *alma mater*, alumni are wielding their money and influence to change curricula and influence academic appointments. Right-wing alumni organizations like Women for Freedom (WFF) and the National Alumni Foundation (NAF) are orchestrating these attacks on campuses across the country. Conservative alumni groups have formed at Princeton, Dartmouth, Duke, Mt. Holyoke, Stanford, Vassar, Washington & Lee, and others.

The Houston-based Women for Freedom is led by Wellesley alumnus Larissa Yanov. The Wellesley WFF newsletter proclaims, "Wellesley's greatness must be forever above extremism as the voice for all." WFF and similar groups receive assistance from the conservative Intercollegiate Studies Institute's Forum for University Stewardship. ISI's quarterly magazine *Campus* claimed in the fall of 1993, "they [alumni] are awakening to the threat radical politicization poses to the integrity of their schools." With few other sources of campus news, alumni are swallowing the contrived myth of "political correctness" as the bane of academic life.

Conservative alumni provide financial support to Right-wing student groups, newspapers, and speakers such as Phyllis Schlafly and Pennsylvania Governor William Casey. But the greatest cause for alarm is that universities are listening obediently to their dollar-backed opinions, as shown recently at a small women's college in South Carolina.

When Ellen Wood-Hall, the first woman President of Converse College, introduced new ideas (i.e. short hair, visitation hours for men, and support-groups for lesbians), alumnae from as far back as 1943 threatened financial withholdings and launched a local media campaign against her. Campus reported that this campaign was intended to retain the "long-standing traditions and character" of Converse College. Hall eventually resigned, stating that she "was attacked for no reason other than being female. I was criticized about my clothes and lack of personal beauty." *(Democratic Culture,* Fall 1995.)

Campus heralded her resignation as the "first known case of trustee inquiry and oversight of politically correct excesses leading to the resignation of top school officials." They praised this "courageous and responsible" act by alumnae as an example of how "higher education could be reformed overnight."

Another significant Right-wing alumni organization is the National Alumni Forum (NAF), founded by former Chair of the National Endowment for the Humanities Lynne Cheney in 1995. Support for NAF came from former Colorado Governor Dick Lamm, Senator Joseph Lieberman (D-Conn.), Senator Hank Brown (R-Col), Jerry Martin, Irving Kristol, Martin Peretz, and Judge Laurence Silberman. NAF has launched a well-funded battle against "political correctness" and multiculturalism, and supports college curriculum changes. In actuality, this is a battle over the right of the wealthy to impose their interests on their alma mater. According to Cheney, it "comes down to the question of who owns the university." *(Memphis Commercial-Appeal,* 3/18/95.)

The National Alumni Forum claims in their mission statement that they are working to preserve and foster "free academic debate and the pursuit of truth." However, in the name of "freedom" they have ousted progressive administrators. To defend "the life and liberty of the mind" they attempted to replace multicultural courses with Western Studies requirements. In promoting "academic excellence" they have assumed control, as Texas oil billionare Lee Bass tried, over the appointment of professors at their colleges. *[See article on next page.]*

Patricia A. McGuire, President of Trinity College in Washington, weathered attacks by alumni who called on graduates to withhold donations to force her resignation. McGuire believes that the conservative attacks prevent academics and others from "participating in a healthy conversation and then moving forward together." She aptly characterizes their position: "'If you don't do what I say, I'm going to trash you forever.' Withholding gifts [and threatening the jobs of administrators] is a form of academic blackmail."

Manufactured News: Yale, Lee Bass, and the Culture Wars

by *Teachers for a Democratic Culture*

The formation of the National Alumni Forum coincided with a national controversy at Yale University. The story, as Newt Gingrich tells it, is this: "Yale University recently had to return $20 million to oil tycoon Lee Bass because after several years the university could not get the faculty to agree to teach Western Civilization." In fact, nothing like this PC fantasy ever happened.

According to the National Alumni Forum, Lee Bass withdrew his $20 million gift to Yale University "after it became clear that his wishes would not be followed." In fact, the gift was returned only after Bass demanded a right to veto faculty appointed to the program whose views he opposed. Rather than criticizing this appalling abuse of the donation process, the National Alumni Forum presents Bass a victim of political correctness, quoting Camille Paglia's claim that "they were dragging their feet because of the content" and *New York Post* columnist Hilton Kramer's declaration that "tenured left-wing advocates of a multiculturalist anti–Western political agenda" were in "open warfare against the creation of the course." (National Alumni Forum newsletter, Fall 1995)

However, this was not a case of "Political Correctness 1, Education 0," as the National Alumni Forum claimed. As David Karp noted in the *Washington Post* (6/4/95), the delays in implementing the Western Culture course had nothing to do with leftist faculty opposing the proposal.

Yale's efforts to start a Western Civilization course were delayed by the administrators' efforts to use the Bass money to offset faculty cuts in the

drawing by Ben Leon

budget. But *Light and Truth,* a conservative student publication funded by the right-wing Intercollegiate Studies Institute (ISI), ran a story by Pat Collins accusing left-wing professors of sabotaging the project. According to Collins, "President Levin obviously made the determination that it was better to be loved by the left wing of his faculty than by his alumni donors."

ISI President T. Kenneth Cribb, Jr., flew to Texas in an effort to convince Bass to withdraw his donation in order to punish Yale. Although Yale promised to implement the program as Bass originally conceived it, Cribb convinced Bass to demand the right to veto any professors hired for the program. Faced with a donor insisting on ideological control over the Western Civilization program, Yale chose to return the money rather than allow academic freedom to be jeopardized. Other alumni donors were inspired to withdraw their gifts. According to Cribb, "The cost of Yale's behavior is now estimated to be several times the original Bass gift of $20 million." *(National Review,* 9/25/95) Yale and other universities now know that they will be punished, and harmed financially, if they fail to implement a conservative agenda.

Lynne Cheney declared about the Bass donation, "It is sad to see politics play any role in deciding what educational opportunities will be available to students." It is indeed sad to see politics playing a major role in the attempts to intimidate and malign Yale University. It is sad to see that conservatives would kill a Western Culture program — blaming its death on the left — and deprive students of the chance to study the West for the sake of gaining more fodder in a propaganda culture war.

[Reprinted with permission from the fall 1995 issue of Democratic Culture, *the newsletter of Teachers for a Democratic Culture.]*

Saving Your Child From 'Raving Marxist Lesbo-Feminists'

by David Kennedy

The *Common-Sense Guide to American Colleges* does not belong on the shelves next to *Barron's Guide to Colleges*. Instead, it should be placed in the Politics/Current Affairs section of the bookstore. The book equates the glorification of Western civilization and conservative politics with educational excellence. It is hard to imagine a more underhanded campaign to persuade the general public that once Johnny gets to college he will be indoctrinated by Marxist scholars, renounce family values, smoke pot, and fornicate with men.

Common Sense?

Produced by the Madison Center for Educational Affairs, the guide equates academic rigor with indoctrination in the Western canon. The book's Dictionary Section defines "fascist" as "anyone who is not politically correct; anyone who advocates capitalism, liberty, and individual rights." They consider Homosexual Studies at Brown nothing more than an "academic fad," label Duke's English department the "best-paid group of nihilists in America," and claim Yale's English department suffers from the "deconstructionist virus."

Underlying assumptions of the book were made clear by Andy Zappia, a primary contributor to the *Guide.* When I asked Zappia why it merited the label "Common Sense," he replied, "Reason is on our side. Truth is on our side. Rationality is on our side. Common sense is on our side." In other words, "Because we say so." Madison Center Vice President Charles Horner also writes in the introduction:

> We feel that there is a relationship between the decline of standards in academic and intellectual life and the growing vulgarity and tastelessness that is increasingly prevalent in American society.

Although the cover of the book says it is "Politically Incorrect," this does not convey the character of the *Guide.* "Politically Incorrect," to most, means that the book does not partake in the caricatured excesses of liberal thought. This label fails to convey the *Guide's* vehement opposition to feminism, Afro-American studies, and multiculturalism.

The Pretext of Scholarly Rigor

Accompanying the discussion of each school, a side box of course descriptions is intended to elicit the reader's dismay at the supposed lack of intellectual substance in its curricula. Courses singled out for ridicule include "English 119 - Feminist Theory, Feminist Practice" at the University of Chicago, "Government 308 - Class, Race, and Interest Groups in US Politics" at Cornell, and "272S - Marxism and Feminism" and "Afro-Am 445 - Comparative Black Political Thought" at the State University of New York at Binghamton.

Their "academic standards" argument is nothing more than a pretext for conservative hostility toward multiculturalism and non-Western curricula. As Zappia admitted to me, the Madison Center would oppose a Marxist history of Latin America no matter how challenging or rigorous. The issue is not standards. The issue is ideology.

"Politics? Us?"

The *Guide* uses simple criteria for judging schools: activism = bad; out homosexuals = bad; Black activists = bad; willingness to confront sexual issues = promiscuous = bad. Two examples illustrate the triumph of ideology over common sense in the publication. The Madison Center writes about a "female freshman" [sic] at Wake Forest University shocked by sexual openness at her school: "[Her] innocence is soon lost as the public discussion of sex, abortion, and AIDS dulls the conscience and emboldens the libido." On the other hand, Princeton's Nude Co-ed Olympics is praised because it "definitely gives a new look to an old tradition, yet the raucous spirit of the event is clearly undiminished." Just as long as they don't talk about AIDS or abortion while they're standing there completely naked.

The *Guide* claims that the aim of multiculturalism is ideological oppression through the elimination of Western values in the curriculum. Multiculturalism constitutes "intellectual McCarthyism," insisted Zappia. He denies that excluding feminism, among other subjects, constitutes McCarthyism, because "There is only liberal McCarthyism. There is no conservative McCarthyism." How's that for common sense?

According to Zappia, the Madison Center does not oppose teaching about other cultures or systems of thought *per se* but believes that it should not be "politicized" by leftist ideologues. So why does the *Guide* consistently mock courses on feminist theory, Marxist theory, or gender and race stratification? Zappia assured me the Madison Center wants a balanced curriculum, like that of St. John's College of Annapolis and Sante Fe. The Madison Center asserts that in a knock-down, no-holds-barred fight between cultures, Western civilization would kick ass.

There is an Alternative

Looking for a progressive alternative to the Madison Center *Common Sense Guide to American Colleges?* Try the new *Multicultural Student's Guide to Colleges*, which provides up-to-date information for students of color. The Guide takes "a critical look at over 200 of America's top schools to see what they offer — both socially and academically." Questions on tenured professors of color, racial diversity and segregation, ethnic studies programs, and administrative responses to crimes of prejudice are explored. Interviews with current students of color about support centers, student organizations, and the political and cultural climate of the campus help give a taste of what it's like at institutions previously for white males only. There's also an up-to-date look at historically black colleges. The Guide was edited by Robert Mitchell, a high school English teacher in New York City, and published by Farrar, Straus and Giroux.

[excerpted with permisson from Perspective: Harvard's Monthly Journal of Liberal Opinion.]

After a Penn State Student condemned misogyny in the mainstream school newspaper, her face was published as part of this centerfold by the Madison Center-funded Lionhearted

ACADEMIC SUPPORT FOR RACISM, SEXISM, HOMOPHOBIA,

ANTI-ENVIRONMENTALISM, AND MILITARISM

drawing by Andy Singer/ National Student News Service

Heterosexual Correctness

by John K. Wilson

Perhaps no group is more persecuted on college campuses than gay, lesbian, and bisexual faculty and students. Deprived of protection under the law, and banned by many colleges, gays and lesbians are still fighting for the right to equality. Many of the same people who condemn "political correctness" are silent about attacks on the rights of gays and lesbians, or are leading the campaign for homophobia.

While fewer gays and lesbians are closeted than in the past and discrimination is less severe than it once was, coming out is still a risk to a teacher's career. Formal discrimination against gay and lesbian faculty has not been eliminated. The worst offenders are religious institutions, but homophobia persists at many secular colleges.

In July 1994, openly lesbian poet Nuala Archer was removed as director of the Cleveland State University Poetry Center after she sponsored a national poetry contest for "all lesbian poets of color" that was funded by a $5,635 grant from the Women's Community Foundation. Her critics claim the firing was due to her poor administration of the Poetry Center. But David Evert of the Poetry Center committee noted, "My only concern was that the last thing we wanted was to have something coming out of CSU that was potentially controversial without some sort of warning." Even if Archer's administrative skills were questionable, the fear of something "controversial" was clearly the major factor in her dismissal. (*Cleveland Plain-Dealer*, 8/9/94)

At the Montana College of Mineral Science and Technology, English professor Henry Gonshak proposed a summer course on "gay and lesbian studies." A fundamentalist pastor in a local church wrote a letter to the newspaper protesting the class title. Gonshak reports, "the alumni soon began besieging Tech administrators with letters and telephone calls. They threatened to withdraw thousands of dollars in contributions unless the class was dropped." (*Democratic Culture*, Spring 1995)

Students supporting gay and lesbian rights are also heavily regulated. Administrators at many colleges encourage homophobia by banning gay and lesbian student groups and in some cases by making homosexuality grounds for expulsion. In 1993, the student government at St. John's

University banned the Gay, Lesbian and Bisexual Alliance for being inconsistent with the institution's religious values, a day after the student group returned from a national march on Washington for gay rights. The administration refused to overturn the decision. (*New York Times*, 5/13/93) Gay and lesbian student groups have also been banned at Notre Dame, Boston College, and several other campuses.

In 1994, administrators at Stephen F. Austin State University over-turned a student government's decision to ban a gay and lesbian student group from campus and revoke its funding because "a group that advocates breaking the law shouldn't be getting student fees." (*Dallas Morning Star,* 11/10/94) In 1991, Auburn's student government refused to charter the Auburn Gay and Lesbian Alliance. After administrators approved the group under threat of an ACLU lawsuit, Alabama passed a law unanimous against using public funds or facilities to support a group that "promotes a lifestyle or actions" prohibited by state sodomy laws. Auburn University requested all student groups to sign a promise not to encourage violations of the state's sodomy law. (*Atlanta Journal-Constitution*, 10/21/92, 8/16/94)

When gay and lesbian activities are supported at public universities, state legislators often intervene and threaten funding. At Indiana University, plans to spend $50,000 on an Office of Gay, Lesbian, and Bisexual Student Support Services were scrapped after a state legislator threatened to cut $500,000 from the university's budget and a wealthy alumnus threatened to withhold a million dollar donation. Instead, the support center will be renamed the Office of Student Ethics and Anti-Harassment Office, and will be funded by private donations. (*Campus Report*, November 1994)

At Kent State University, the College Republicans protested allowing a class on the sociology of gays and lesbians to be taught, arguing that offering the class to students was tantamount to University sanctioning of the gay lifestyle. In 1993, before the course was ever taught, an Ohio state senator wrote to Kent State President Carol Cartwright, threatening to cut state funding if it was permitted. (*Campus Report*, November 1994) The interference of state legislators in university affairs poses a dramatic threat to academic freedom, particularly when their goal is to silence gays and lesbians.

[Excerpted with permission from Democratic Culture, *the newsletter of Teachers for a Democratic Culture, Fall 1995.]*

Female Anti-Feminism:
3 Easy Steps to Fame and Profit!

by Jennifer L. Pozner

1. Claim you are a feminist.

Use Leftist lingo to gain rebellious credibility in a supposedly politically correct culture. Insist you care about women's equality and strength, but you resent the "victim mindset" espoused by 90's feminists. Become vocally indignant at their refusal to tolerate your "dissenting feminist voice." Use your role as "rebel feminist" to denounce every feminist concern other than women's economic advancement.

2. Denounce all other feminists.

Blast feminists as willfully distorting statistics and facts to garner support for their various causes. Denounce feminist scholarship as overly ideological and non-academic. Then substantiate your claims by using faulty research methods and superficial interviews. Rarely contact the authors, activists and psychologists you libel.

3. Take a lesson from Monopoly.

Go directly to the media. Do not pass up the college lecture circuit. Do not turn down close to $200K in Right Wing grants.

Wait for the money to come rolling in.

I wish the preceding section was merely satire. Unfortunately, the how-to guide above could very easily be a synopsis of the methodology employed by Christina Hoff Sommers in *Who Stole Feminism?: How Women Have Betrayed Women*. Sommers believes that the battle against sexism has been waged and duly won; therefore, since sexism is a thing of the past, feminists are fighting against imaginary problems. Sommers insists she wrote her 1994 book "because I am a feminist who does not like what feminism has become." She then offers up an across-the-board condemnation of almost every influential activist, scholar, agency and study of the second wave feminist movement.

To Sommers, "gender feminists" (the label she gives to activists and writers such as Gloria Steinem, Patricia Ireland and Susan Faludi, who believe that sexism is still a pervasive and detrimental force in this society) are proponents of a "divisive and resentful philosophy [which] adds to the woes of our society and hurts legitimate feminism." She believes that feminist academics have created doctrinairian women's studies programs which "shortchange women students... waste their time, give them bad intellectual habits... [and] isolate them socially and academically." According to Sommers, "overzealous" young women "bemuse and alarm the public with inflated statistics" when they attempt to prosecute as a rapist and gender bigot "a boy getting fresh in the backseat of a car." Feminists who target anorexia, bulimia and dangerous standards of feminine beauty practice "alarmist advocacy." Sommers dismisses studies which prove high rates of wife-battering, calls campaigns against sexual harassers "witch hunts," and attacks the American Association of University Women's *Shortchanging Girls, Shortchanging America*, which found that girls' self-esteem suffers as a result of encountering gender bias in the classroom.

Sommers, who teaches philosophy at Clark University, is one of many woman who has appropriated the feminist label to denounce campus feminism as intellectually and socially stifling to women. In her 1993 book *The Morning After: Sex, Fear and Feminism on Campus*, Katie Roiphe ridicules "rape crisis feminists" as neurotic leaders of a cult of female victimization in which women "celebrate their vulnerability [and] accept, even embrace, the mantle of victim status." According to Roiphe, campus feminists are irrational, fading flowers who exaggerate statistics about violence against women in attempt to scare us back to the prudery of the '50's. In a 1993 *Mother Jones* article, Karen Lehrman blasted women's studies programs as offering only "classroom therapy" and "mere pit stops at the academic." *Newsweek's* Sarah Crichton claims that campus feminism is "not creating a society of Angry Young Women. These are Scared Little Girls." Though packaged in bizarrely pro-woman terminology about women's responsibility to take control of their sexuality and stop "wallowing in oppression," it is not hard to find the misogyny implicit in these critiques. In a *Newsweek* article entitled "Stop Whining," right-wing commentator and former Republican speech writer Mary Matalin proposed this solution to placate young feminist "crackpots": "Give these moody girls a prescription of Motrin and some water pills, quick!"

drawing
by Ben Leon

In an essay about rape activism in *Who Stole Feminism?*, Sommers retells Roiphe's main premise: that feminists are reinforcing the oppression of women by constantly speaking about misogynistic violence. Roiphe writes that feminists, "preoccupied" with date rape and campus harassment, "produce endless images of women as victims — women offended by a professor's dirty joke, women pressured into sex by peers, women trying to say no but not managing to get it across." Killing the messengers seems to be Roiphe's semantic game of choice. Feminists do not *produce* images of female victimization, rather we *expose* atrocities done to women so as to make them unacceptable, with the end goal being the elimination of violence against women. A date-rape survivor was not "pressured into sex by a peer," she was *forced* into sex against her will. And how would Roiphe have a woman whose protests were willfully disregarded manage to more convincingly "get no across" to a rapist? By blaming campus feminists for glorifying the victimization they are fundamentally against, these critics shift the responsibility for the violation of women onto the women who are fighting abuse.

These critics' right to speak *for* feminists *as* feminists has rarely been challenged by the media. Quite the contrary: the *New York Times* praised Roiphe for her "courage" in speaking against the feminist party line, and a *Boston Globe* review of *Who Stole Feminism?* was titled "Rebel in the Sisterhood." Katie Roiphe insists *The Morning After* was written "out of the deep belief that some feminisms are better than others." Roiphe says she wants women to take control, and that she resents "rape crisis feminists" for teaching women to be prudes and therefore denying women's sexual agency. Yet how can someone who consistently mocks rape survivors who tell of their attacks, calling them "naive," "melodramatic," "excessive," and "paranoid," honestly claim to be concerned about women's sexual rights and pleasure?

And one must question the motives of a "feminist" such as Sommers, who has been quoted in *Esquire* as saying, "There are a lot of homely women in women's studies. Preaching these anti-male, anti-sex sermons is a way for them to compensate for various heartaches — they're just mad at the beautiful girls." By that standard, Laura Flanders notes in *EXTRA!*, Rush "Feminism was established so as to allow unattractive women easier access to the mainstream of society" Limbaugh is a feminist. Sommers would probably be flattered if told she resembled Limbaugh, who has repeatedly plugged *Who Stole Feminism* on his radio show as "a brave and courageous book." In response, Sommers told Limbaugh, the man who coined the term *Femi-nazi*, "I am proud you like the book."

Anti-feminist women who attack feminism under the guise of the liberal cause of women's advancement are far less easy to dismiss than right-wing critics such as Phyllis Schlafly or Rush Limbaugh. Yet Schlafly and Sommers are both listed in the speakers guide of the Young Americas Foundation, a group which routinely gives $10K grants to student groups to bring conservative lecturers to their campuses. Sommers is also a speaker for the Intercollegiate Studies Institute, another right think tank, which dishes out the dollars to sponsor lecturers who "counter the Marxists, radical feminists, deconstructionists, and other 'politically correct' types on your campus." The media seize the rhetoric of self-proclaimed "feminist dissenters" such as Sommers and Rophie as proof that feminism is failing women ("See," we are supposed to think, "even the feminists now admit their movement is passé"). They are compensated highly for their complicity: Sommers received over $164,000 in grants from the conservative Olin, Bradley and Carthage foundations for *Who Stole Feminism*, in addition to a six-figure advance from her publisher, Simon and Schuster.

Some questions arise in response to Roiphe's smug assertion that "some feminisms are better than others." Which "brands" of feminism should be considered beneficial to women, and which should be discounted? Whose "feminism" should we trust: the feminism of young activists who lead self-defense workshops, staff battered women's shelters and rape hotlines, push for anti-discrimination legislation, and study and teach women's history, or that of ideologically Right "feminist dissenters" such as Sommers and Roiphe, who constantly mock young women as neo-Victorian wimps? The answer is simple — using Leftist lingo does not make the package any less conservative. Sommers' and Roiphe's "feminisms" consist of one overriding premise: that activists for women's rights are intellectually and sexually naive, and should not be taken seriously when they speak in the classroom or of the bedroom. This is classic backlash fare, and should be dismissed as such. Feminism, in its most pure form, is an ideological movement for women's political, social, and economic equality. These goals — along with complete sexual autonomy for women — form the vision of contemporary campus feminists. Their agenda, not faux-feminists' distorted picture of their movement, is the version of feminism that is truly "better than others."

Uncovering the "Black Conservative" Movement

by Justin Roberts

Polls show that black Americans are consistently more liberal than white Americans on issues involving poverty and race-relations. However, black conservatives are often highlighted as spokespeople for Black America. For example, Star Parker gives conservative speeches on campuses around the country and is listed in the Young America's Foundation guide as "one of the nation's top new leaders in representing black Americans." How could a black conservative speaker claim to represent most black Americans, who are liberal? The answer: money, power, and media coverage.

Monetary Support for Black Conservatives

One reason for the prevalence of black conservative voices on campus and in the media is the monetary support they receive from conservative organizations. In 1975, Thomas Sowell published *Race and Economics*, and according to Cornell West, began a "visible and aggressive" black conservative movement. Sowell's research and writing, particularly against affirmative action, has been primarily funded by the Hoover Institution on War, Revolution, and Peace, a conservative think tank at Stanford University.

According to the Political Research Associates, many other white conservative organizations fund black conservatives. Included in this group are the American Enterprise Institute, the Heritage Foundation (which has even implemented a minority outreach program), the Olin Foundation, the Scaife Foundation, and the Bradley Foundation. On campus, the Young America's Foundation is a primary supporter of black conservative speakers. For the past few years, YAF has sponsored "alternative black speakers" like Clarence Thomas, J.A. Parker, and Walter Williams to speak on topics such as, "How Liberalism Helped Destroy the Moral Fabric that Produced the Civil Rights Movement," "Welfare: 20th Century Slavery," "Affirmative Action Follies," "The Truth About Multiculturalism," and "Failures of Affirmative Action Policies on Campus and in the Nation."

Stephen Carter, in *Reflections of an Affirmative Action Baby,* provides a reason for this rash of monetary support to black conservatives. "When the black folks get out of hand... many white folks think that it is nice to have another black person to shut them down." This is especially the case when the issue is race relations. White conservatives like to have black people denounce affirmative action, welfare, and multiculturalism because blacks are less likely to be called racist and because it makes their platform appear more legitimate; hence the bounty of monetary support for the likes of Sowell.

The Illusion of a Large Black Conservative Movement

In choosing which black speakers to highlight, conservative groups are not particular about academic credentials. The Young America's Foundation sponsored an international relations expert (Alan Keyes) to speak on "How Liberalism Helped Destroy the Moral Fabric of the Civil Rights Movement," a government professor (William Allen) to speak on "The Truth About Multiculturalism," and a marketing major (Star Parker) to speak on "Race Relations in America." Other black speakers promoted by the Foundation emphasized law and economics. Not one of the Foundation's "alternative black speakers" on race-related issues specialized in race relations.

This is just one example where black Americans are taken out of their areas of expertise to act as "experts" on race relations. This adds to the racist idea that black Americans can only be experts on race and contributes to the illusion of a large black conservative movement.

Both liberal and conservative black organizations are supported by white foundations. However, the major difference between the two groups is their constituency. Liberal black organizations usually reflect the ideas of the majority of black Americans, while conservative black organizations find their support, funding, and the origins of their ideas within the ranks of the white conservative movement. Both claim to represent the views of black America, and both receive media coverage and support for speaking tours. However, only one group has a large constituency within black America: black liberals. The large black conservative constituency is merely an illusion.

Conservative Organizations and Individuals

Although black conservative thought is widely overrepresented in the media, some influential organizations and individuals deserve mention. One organization is the Lincoln Institute, which was described in *The Public Eye* as "the bastion of black conservatism." Another is Black PAC which, according to Political Research Associates, "worked for Jesse

Helms's re-election, and to oppose the 'terrorist outlaw' African National Congress and 'extremists' such as Jesse Jackson and the Congressional Black Caucus."

Black conservative publications include *National Minority Politics*, *Diversity and Division*, and *The Lincoln Review*, a quarterly publication by the Lincoln Institute. Political Research Associates described *The Lincoln Review* as "anti-choice, pro-death penalty, anti-affirmative action, pro-defense spending, anti-Martin Luther King national holiday, pro-school prayer, anti-Washington D.C. statehood...and uncritically supportive of Israel."

Individual representatives of these organizations include Clarence Thomas, a member of the advisory board for *The Lincoln Review* from 1981 to 1990; William Keyes, the founder of Black PAC; and J.A. Parker, past treasurer of Black PAC, current president of the Lincoln Institute, and current editor of *The Lincoln Review*.

These organizations and individuals represent a minority of the views held by black Americans on issues like welfare, affirmative action, and multiculturalism. However, their money, power, and media coverage lends the illusion of a large black conservative movement. Progressive individuals and organizations should see through the subterfuge and continue to challenge conservative dogma, regardless of what color the spokespersons happen to be.

The Southern League:
Providing Academic Legitimacy to a New Confederate Movement

by John Keeble

Rooted in what is known as the Deep South, the state of Alabama is still a jagged edge in the world. Powerful historical forces—the black and the white, an old Southern economy and the new Atlanta-based one—converge here. The Confederate battle flag, made over into the insignia of white supremacy, is resurgent. The Southern League, a three-year-old organization based in Tuscaloosa, uses it as the standard under which a case for a revitalized Southern white identity can be made.

The Southern League argues for a '90s-style, Right-wing, race-and religion-based nationalism that is intended to lead to secession from the union. The Southern League opposes welfare, affirmative action, "the enormity of multiculturalism," and multinational corporations. It embraces what its president, Michael Hill, terms "organic traditionalism," and the "proud legacy of [the South's] Anglo-Celtic civilization," or a kind of heroic Cracker Culture, which is an epithet league members take up proudly from a book of the same title by the prominent Southern historian and Southern League board member, Grady McWhiney.

Indeed, the league's leadership is composed of the likes of McWhiney and Thomas Fleming, editor of *Chronicles: A Magazine of American Culture*. These are figures drawn from a growing number of academics Michael Hill describes as "a Southern literati and intelligentisia." It becomes clear that what is important about the league is its leadership's capacity for weaving an elaborate white man's dream world, or mythology. Within it the pent-up anger and potential for violence of a less articulate constituency can be housed. By hiding race hatred behind a sophisticated facade, the Southern League has the possibility of emerging as a potent national force.

Founded in Tuscaloosa in 1994, the Southern League soon grew, according to Hill, to 1200 members and 10 chapters throughout the South. Following the installation of a web site in 1995, its ranks mushroomed in several months to more than 3000. Chapters now exist in 26 states, including California and Arizona, Montana, and Texas. The league holds annual conferences and is planning to put a Cultural and

Educational Institute at an antebellum plantation in rural South Carolina.

Being an ideological organization with intellectual ambitions, the Southern League recruits at universities. A controversy at the University of Alabama began with the efforts of the league's student chapter to obtain university funding as an educational organization. The chapter discouraged Eric Perkins, the lone black student who dared to attend its meetings, from continuing to come after he questioned the members' habit of referring to the Civil War as the War for Southern Independence. The group requested that the university create a Southern Studies Program staffed by faculty educated in the South. When it appeared that funding would be denied, chapter president Findlay threatened suit and issued a set of demands that included a specially designated Confederate Heritage Week, provisions for the university's marching bad to perform "Dixie" at home games, and for Southern League members to fly the Confederate flag at all sporting events under the protection of university police.

In November, the public relations officer of the Southern League student chapter, Thomas Stedham, published two letters in the student newspaper, the *Crimson White*, that mocked affirmative action and cited *Bell Curve*-style statistics on African American crime rates and educational testing performances. Meanwhile, Findlay threatened English professor Diane Roberts (according to Roberts), a Southerner, for "indoctrinating her students with a Yankee view of Southern heritage. The Southern League student chapter was finally advised that it would not be eligible for funding on the grounds that it was a political organization.

Many faculty and students as well as citizens across the state are outraged by the Southern League's agenda. "They dress up the message of the Klan, the skinheads, the Aryan nations," Pat Hermann (UA English faculty) told me. "(T)hey appear slightly better groomed than the Klan, better tailored, and better educated. For that reason, critical discourse with them resembles a rational discourse with Herr Himmler on a population problem in Germany."

[Excerpted with permission from The Village Voice, *June 11, 1996.]*

Sellout Scientists:
Industry-Funded Skeptics Undermine Global Warming Consensus

by Ross Gelbspan

Even as global warming intensifies, the evidence is being denied with a ferocious disinformation campaign. This campaign is waged on many fronts: in the media, where public opinion is formed; in the halls of Congress, where laws are made; and in international climate negotiations. In their most important accomplishment, global warming critics have successfully created the general perception that scientists are sharply divided over whether it is taking place at all.

Key to this success has been the effective use of a tiny band of scientists — principally Drs. Patrick Michaels, Sherwood Idso, Robert Balling, and S. Fred Singer — who have proven extraordinarily adept at draining the issue of all sense of crisis. Deep-pocketed industry public relations specialists have promoted their opinions through every channel of communication they can reach. They have demanded access to the press for these scientists' views, as a right of journalistic fairness.

Unfortunately, most editors are too uninformed about climate science to resist. They would not accord to tobacco company scientists who dismiss the dangers of smoking the same weight that they accord to world-class lung specialists. But in the area of climate research, few major news stories fail to feature prominently one of these handful of industry-sponsored scientific "greenhouse skeptics."

If the public has been lulled into a state of disinterest, the effect on decision makers has been even more effective. Testimony by industry-sponsored skeptics contributed to the defeat of proposals to increase the cost of fossil-fuel generated power, to cut the climate research budget, and to discredit the scientific findings of the UN's Intergovernmental Panel of Climate Change (IPCC), which represents the consensus of 2,500 scientists.

The rise to prominence of most of these greenhouse skeptics is spelled out in several reports of the Western Fuels Association, a Washington, DC-based nonprofit consortium of coal utilities and suppliers. In its 1994 annual report, Western Fuels declared that "there has been a close to universal impulse in the [fossil fuel] trade association community here in Washington to concede the scientific premise of global warming...

We have disagreed, and do disagree, with this strategy."

To counter it, the group said it would support the work of those who challenged the findings of the world's leading scientists. Among them: Dr. Pat Michaels, associate professor of climatology at the University of Virginia; Dr. S. Fred Singer, also of UVA; and Dr. Robert Balling, director of the climatology program at Arizona State University.

Dr. Pat Michaels calls his industry-funded publications serious journals of climate science. However, he ignores the fact that all research sponsored by the federal government is subjected to the exacting requirements of scientific proof through a system of review by other experts. By contrast, Michaels' research is frequently published in industry journals without undergoing this kind of rigorous scientific scrutiny. Michaels has even referenced articles by E. Keith Idso, son of greenhouse skeptic Dr. Sherwood Idso, which were later published in the *New American,* the newsletter of the John Birch Society. (*World Climate Review,* Volume 1, Number 4.)

Witness this passage by Michaels in the Fall 1994 issue of *World Climate Review:* "The fact is that the artifice of climate-change-apocalypse is crumbling faster than Cuba... There is genuine fear in the environmental community about this one, for the decline and fall of such a prominent issue is sure to horribly maim the credibility of the green movement that espoused it so cheerily."

In the winter 1993 issue, he wrote of government-sponsored climate research scientists: "The fact is that virtually every successful academic scientist is a ward of the federal government. One cannot do the research necessary to publish enough to be awarded tenure without appealing to one or another agency for considerable financial support... Yet these and other agencies have their own political agendas."

By attacking these scientists as politically motivated, Michaels succeeded in having his testimony judged as credible by the House Science Committee, and was able to help secure funding cuts for programs to study the global climate.

In May 1995 testimony under oath to the Minnesota Public Utilities Commission, Michaels revealed under oath that he had received more than $165,000 in industry and private funding over the previous five years. Not only did Western Fuels fund two journals that he edited — his *World Climate Review* and its successor newsletter *World Climate Report* — but it provided a $63,000 grant for his research. Another $49,000 came to Michaels from the German Coal Mining Association and $15,000 from the Edison Electric Institute. Michaels also listed a grant of $40,000 from the western mining company Cyprus Minerals, the largest single funder of the anti-environmental Wise Use movement.

It is quite extraordinary that with such ties, Michael's testimony at congressional hearings chaired by Rep. Robert Walker (R-Pa.) and Rep. Dana Rohrabacher (R-Calif.) was accorded more weight than that of four internationally renowned climate scientists.

The case of Dr. Robert Balling is equally intriguing. A geographer by training, much of Balling's research focused on hydrology, precipitation, water runoff and other Southwestern water and soil-related issues until he was solicited by Western Fuels. Balling has since emerged as one of the most visible and prolific of the climate-change skeptics.

Since 1991, Balling has received, either alone or with colleagues, nearly $300,000 from coal and oil interests in research funding, which he also disclosed for the first time at the Minnesota hearing. In his collaborations with Sherwood Idso, Balling has received about $50,000 from Cyprus, $80,000 from German Coal and $75,000 from British Coal Corp. Two Kuwaiti government foundations have given him a $48,000 grant and unspecified consulting fees and have published his 1992 book, "The Heated Debate," in Arabic. The book was originally published by a conservative think tank, the Pacific Research Institute, one of whose goals is the repeal of environmental regulations.

Among the skeptics, Professor S. Fred Singer stands out for being consistently forthcoming about his funding by large oil interests and conservative groups. Singer is director of the Science and Energy Policy Project at the University of Virginia. During a 1994 appearance on ABC's "Nightline," Singer did not deny having received funding from the Rev. Sun Myung Moon (to whose newspaper, the *Washington Times,* he is a regular contributor and whose organization has published three of his books). Nor has he apologized for his funding from Exxon, Shell, ARCO, Unocal and Sun Oil. Singer's defense is that his scientific position on global atmospheric issues predates that funding and has not changed because of it.

And it is true that Singer held firm to a similar position on another environmental controversy — despite overwhelming evidence against his position. Singer once warned the oil companies that they face the same threat as the chemical firms that produced chlorofluorocarbons (CFCs), a class of chemicals that was found to be depleting the earth's protective ozone layer. "It took only five years to go from... mandating a simple freeze of production [of CFCs] at 1985 levels, to the 1992 decision of a complete production phase-out — all on the basis of quite insubstantial science," Singer wrote.

Contrary to his assertion virtually all relevant researchers say the link between CFCs and ozone depletion rests on unassailable scientific evidence. As if to underscore the point, the three scientists who discovered the CFC-ozone link were awarded the Nobel Prize for chemistry. But that did not faze Singer, who proceeded to attack the Nobel committee in the Washington Times. Singer's tantrum against the Nobel committee would be laughable — except that his views are influential, especially with conservative politicians. Based in part on Singer's work, House Majority Whip Tom DeLay (R-Tex.) and Rep. John Doolittle (R-Calif.) are making an effort to withdraw U.S. participation in the Montreal Protocol, the international compact that mandates an end to production of the chemicals that destroy the ozone layer. Despite the remarkable international consensus on the Montreal Protocol, DeLay used Singer's pronouncements to attribute it merely to "a media scare."

[Excerpted with permission from The Heat is On, *by Ross Gelbspan, published by Addison Wesley Longman, May 1997.]*

"PATRIOT-ISM" AT TUFTS

by Erin Bush

Dr. Theodore Postol of MIT created a few waves in the Defense Establishment in 1992. Postol had the nerve to suggest that the Patriot missile, the gem of the Gulf War that pushed Raytheon into the national spotlight, did not work as well as the public was led to believe.

In April of 1992, Postol delivered the results of his analysis to the House Armed Services Committee. Postol's research led him to conclude that "if we had not attempted to defend against Scuds, the level of resulting damage would be no worse than what actually occurred."[1] These few words were enough to start a full-scale campaign against Postol and his research.

Up to this point, the Patriot stood as a shining example of the U.S. mastery of high-tech warfare. On January 30, 1991, General Schwarzkopf declared that the Patriot had been launched against 33 Scud missiles and had hit every one. In March of 1991, the Army raised the statistic to 45 hits out of 47 attempts. Raytheon then proudly declared that their product had destroyed almost 90% of scuds in Saudi Arabia, and 50% in Israel. Soon everyone wanted the Patriot. Raytheon started to receive orders for the missile from all over the world. Potential revenues reached into the billions. In addition, Raytheon seemed likely to receive lucrative governmental contracts for upgraded versions of the missile defense system.

Charles M. Perry, Vice President and Director of Studies at the Cambridge-based Institute for Foreign Policy Analysis (IFPA), echoed the thoughts of many when he stated that the Patriot performed so well that it could change the whole outlook of American defense. In September of 1991, Perry declared that "ever since those first dramatic Patriot intercepts over Tel Aviv, Riyad, and Daharan, the very notion of foregoing greater investment in missile defense... seems absurd."[2]

Meanwhile, Postol continued to dispute these claims. In a January 1992 article in *International Security* (a Harvard-based peer-reviewed journal) he described using television footage to document the Patriot's "almost total failure to intercept quite primitive attacking missiles."[3]

Raytheon led an all-out attack. A litany of unsubstantiated claims against Postol's professional credentials soon flooded the local media. Postol found himself fighting attempts to revoke his security clearance, a temporary gag order that forbade him from mentioning the word "Patriot", and charges that he faked his data. In addition, Postol's department lost a total of $25,000 in funding from Mitre (a non-profit laboratory specializing in Defense research) and Martin Marietta (a subcontractor of Raytheon). Postol explains that "The issue, to me, is that a large Corporation was thuggishly attacking an individual, both personally and professionally, and that the [MIT] Administration did not support that individual, but actually saddled up to that Corporation."

drawing by Ben Leon

Certainly, the MIT administration had its reasons for discouraging this political controversy. MIT has enjoyed a close relationship with Raytheon ever since Vannevar Bush (then an associate professor of electrical engineering at the school) helped form Raytheon in 1922. In the past 50 years Raytheon has donated $4.7 million to MIT.

One of Postol's critics was Mr. Robert L. Pfaltzgraff whose scathing attack was published in the Wall Street Journal on April 8, 1992. In this op-ed piece, Pfaltzgraff asserted that the Patriot "successfully engaged" 60% of the scuds encountered, and that the information that Postol used in their analysis was flawed. He asserted that the Patriot's performance had revolutionized America's conception of defense.

The biography at the end of the letter described Pfaltzgraff as a professor of international security studies at Tufts University's Fletcher School of Law and Diplomacy. The fact that Pfaltzgraff was, and remains, President of the Cambridge-based Institute for Foreign Policy Analysis (IFPA), a conservative think-tank which receives funding from Raytheon, was conspicuously absent from this article. As a matter of fact, the IFPA as a whole seemed rather taken with Raytheon's product.

Pfaltzgraff's sales pitch makes more sense once you dig a bit deeper into the IFPA. In fiscal year 1991, Raytheon's Missile Systems Division donated $60,000 to the IFPA. Charles F. Adams, an ex-CEO of Raytheon who now chairs the finance committee of its board of directors, also serves on the board of the IFPA.

The Fletcher School of Law and Diplomacy, which is associated with the IFPA, also has a cozy relationship with Raytheon. Here, Charles Adams serves as the Chairman of the Board of Visitors (he is also a Trustee Emeritus of Tufts). Tufts has also received generous contributions from Mr. Adams and an undisclosed amount from both the Charles F. Adams Charitable Trust and Raytheon.

Although this situation does raise some serious questions about a possible conflict of interest, this is only the beginning of the story.

Commies, Money and the IFPA

The IFPA started operations in 1976 with the largest single seed grant, $325,000, ever given by the Scaife Family Trust [4], to stress "the danger of international communism and the need for a strong defense for the United States."[5] The Scaife conglomerate remains a generous supporter of the IFPA, donating $385,000 in fiscal year 1991, as well as the Fletcher School.[6] The John M. Olin Foundation, the Lynde and Harry Bradley Foundation, the Center for National Program Evaluation, and the William H. Donner Foundation also support the IFPA.

Many prime weapons contractors contribute to the IFPA as well. Other than Raytheon, Rockwell International, McDonnell Douglas, Westinghouse, G.T.E., and Boeing Aerospace are all patrons. The Defense Nuclear Agency and the Department of the Navy also awarded grants to the Institute in F.Y. 1991. All in all, these contributions and grants supplied $1.5 million for the Institute yearly.

The philosophy of the IFPA has been described as "frankly hawkish." Their topics of study have included how the U.S. can retaliate against a nuclear strike, how cruise missiles should be deployed, and how the U.S. can protect its land-based missiles.[7]

The international spectrum has changed considerably since 1976, with the "threat" of international communism now rather weak, so perhaps we should feel a bit sorry for these guys. Give them a pat on the back, hand them a gold watch, and let them take a rest from all of that "protection" they have been providing?

Nothing of the sort! These are resourceful people. They have found a new enemy: international arms control. A 1990 IFPA annual report explains that "Emphasis is placed on the need to both anticipate and to preclude arms control accords that would prevent needed modernization."[8] (Perhaps this includes funding for the Patriot and its spin-offs?)

The Institute's 1990 annual report explains how "drawing upon its extensive network of research consultants and overseas contacts, the IFPA team has provided clients and contracting agencies with "strategic" assessments in the area of defense cooperation, including market analyses."[9] This is a cryptic statement, but when you consider who the clients and contracting agencies of the Institute are, it also becomes rather interesting. Just what kind of international "market analysis" would a weapons manufacturer need?

Just How Influential Are These Guys?

The IFPA holds numerous conferences, workshops, and seminars all over the world to affect the opinions of top policymakers. These events often attract both US and international policymakers. One such workshop sponsored by the Institute was held in Washington DC in October 1989 and was entitled "Theater Nuclear Forces in a Changing Political, Budgetary, and Arms Control Environment." The Chairman of the House Armed Services Committee, the Under-Secretary of Defense for Acquisition, and the Senior Director for Defense Policy and Arms Control at the National Security Council attended this event.

IFPA-sponsored seminars, such as the "The Rush to Disarm: Maintaining Strategic Deterrence in a Changing Era" (Washington, March 1990) are focused more exclusively on the U.S. Congress. The IFPA held thirty-eight Breakfast Seminars alone in a 1989-90.[10]

The Institute's annual report is full of photographs of members of the IFPA advising former President Bush, General Brent Scowcroft, and Sam Nunn, among others. A letter from Bush excerpted in their annual report: states, "Many thanks... for that session at Kennebunkport which I found most interesting and helpful."[11] Apparently, this Institute has been successful in catching the ear of Washington.

The IFPA has also been able to attract many policymakers into its organization. The board of directors reads like a membership roster of the Reagan and Nixon Administrations: Caspar Weinberger (Reagan's Secretary of Defense and council to the Nixon Administration), Peter Dailey (coordinator of Reagan's "public diplomacy" effort to persuade Europe to accept deployment of Pershing II missiles, and member of the "November Group" of Nixon's Committee to Reelect the President), and Frank Carlucci (Deputy Director of the CIA under Reagan, National Security Advisor to Reagan, and Deputy Weinberger during the Nixon Administration). Pfaltzgraff served on Reagan's advisory team on foreign policy and intelligence during the 1980 campaign.[12]

The IFPA's Board of Research Consultants includes three ex-members of the National Security Council, three members of the Executive Committee of the Committee on the Present Danger (including the Chairman), and two top National Security Advisors to Reagan. These people can only help maintain the prestige of the group.

A Shadowy Relationship with the NSPA

The Institute for Foreign Policy Analysis shares office space with a group called the National Security Planning Associates, Inc. (NSPA). IFPA President Pfaltzgraff, Vice President Charles Perry, and Treasurer Robert Herber all serve on the board of directors of NSPA. This situation gives the term "interlocking directorates" a whole new meaning.

According to its tax returns on public record at the Attorney General's Office in Massachusetts, the non-profit IFPA lists NSPA (a for-profit company) as a "related party" to whom the IFPA furnished $164,687 in fiscal year 1991. This includes a $141,000 loan and $3,000 "investment." Strangely enough, in the same year, the NSPA sold 300,000 shares of penny stock, worth $3,000, to an undisclosed party. This situation suggests a financial relationship between the two organizations that most boards of directors would not allow. It makes one wonder if the foundations that have been supporting the IFPA are aware that the Institute is siphoning such a considerable sum of money into a for-profit group.

The Connection to Academia

Perhaps the most disturbing aspect of this whole story is the effect that IFPA and its supporters have on academia. Pfaltzgraff is considered to be an expert on arms control and lectures at Tufts on that topic. Given his apparent political bent, one wonders how well he can deliver a neutral presentation of the issues surrounding arms control accords. One could also wonder how this man has time to teach at all. Besides lecturing, Pfaltzgraff devotes 35 hours a week to the IFPA[13] and an undisclosed amount of time to his post as a Board member at the NSPA, and he serves on the Board of Advisors of the Naval War College.

It is also interesting to note that a Pfaltzgraff Professorship is endowed by Shelly Cullom Davis, an investment banker and former chair of the Heritage Foundation and the National Right to Work Committee, as well as a member of the Board of Directors at Stanford's Hoover Institution and the Fletcher School. His wife, Kathryn Davis, serves on the IFPA's Board of Directors.

The close financial ties between defense contractors and universities has developed a serious threat to academic freedom. In the past decade, cuts in federal and state non-military funding have forced colleges and universities to find alternative means of funding their research. Many professors have discovered that the Department of Defense (DOD) and its contractors offer the most lucrative grants. Unfortunately, this money usually comes with many strings attached. Professors are penalized for any behavior that could place their patron in a bad light, regardless of the accuracy of their research. The DOD even penalizes other researchers who dispute the results of researchers it funds. This situation effectively stifles debate among many of our nation's top intellectuals.

When funding comes either from the DOD or its contractors, professors are also often forced to operate under the burdens of classification, or pre-publication "review." When funders have the power to censor reports before they are published, or deny professors access by revoking the security clearances of those who do not cooperate, the whole system of peer review collapses. This situation invites shoddy research and lures professors into collusion with the private weapons industry.

Theodore Postol summed up the potential dangers well when he said, "Many of the foundations that fund us have their own political perspective and if you stray too far from that perspective, they will stop funding you." Referring to the grants from military contractors, he adds, "it is no accident that Pfaltzgraff gets funding while I don't. Nobody is going to pay me to go rain on their parade."[14]

[Erin Bush interned at CCO's predecessor, the University Conversion Project.]

Notes

[1]Golden, Daniel. "Missile-blower" *The Boston Globe Magazine*. July 19, 1992, p. 17.
[2]Perry, Charles M. "Theater Missile Threats and Defense Options in the 1990's", The *Annals of the American Academy of Political Science*. Pfaltzgraff, Robert, ed. Sage Publications; Newbury Park, CA, September 1991, p. 79.
[3]Ibid. p. 18.
[4]Saloma, John S. *Ominous Politics*. Farrar, Straus, and Giroux: NY. 1984, p. 29.
[5]*Ominous Politics*, p. 20.
[6]According to their annual report, the Sara Scaife Foundation donated $225,000 to the Fletcher School in 1990.
[7]Williams, Dennis; Abamson, Pamela; and Fineman, Howard. "Idea Factories of the Right" *Newsweek*. December 1, 1980, pp. 35-36.
[8]*Institute for Foreign Policy Analysis Annual Report*, 1990. p. 10.
[9]Ibid. p. 11.
[10]1990 *IFPA Annual Report*, pp. 26-33.
[11]*Institute for Foreign Policy Analysis Annual Report*, 1990 p. 6.
[12]Roosa, John. "Tufts University: Students Counter Spys," *The National Reporter*. Winter 1985, Vol. 9, No. 1; p. 33.
[13]According to the 990 tax form of the IFPA for fiscal year 1991, Robert Pfaltzgraff averaged 35 hours of work weekly, and received a salary of $150,912, as well as $23,592 in benefits.
[14]Interview of Theodore Postol by Erin Bush, August 1992.

ORGANIZING AGAINST

THE CAMPUS CONSERVATIVE AGENDA

Terry Laban/In These Times

Common Questions and Answers About Challenging the Right

by Rich Cowan and Dalya Massachi

1) Do you advocate prohibiting ideas which are not "politically correct"?

There is nothing wrong with influencing opinions. As progressive activists, the challenge is to influence people with facts rather than coercion. Involving people who have historically been ignored in the political process is the responsibility of progressive organizers.

All of these activities are attacked as "censorship" by those accustomed to monopolizing the stage and dominating the decision-making process. It is both ridiculous and dangerous to compare progressive organizing activities to the historical legacies of colonialism and white male supremacy. The danger in the "anti-PC" campaign is that privileged groups will label challenges to their privilege as "fascism" in order to justify a violent response.

Conservative groups have repeatedly indicated a goal of eliminating liberalism and the left. Jack Abramoff, former chair of the College Republicans (CRs), went so far as to say, "we are not just trying to win the next election. We're winning the next generation... It's not our job to seek peaceful co-existence with the Left. Our job is to remove them from power permanently." (*CR 1983 Annual Report*)

2) By talking so much about the Right, aren't you labeling people and creating an "Us vs. Them" dynamic that only breeds violence?

Identifying and naming the oppressor is fundamentally different from using the oppressor's coercive tactics as an instrument of rebellion. We favor the former, and oppose the latter. As long as power hierarchies exist, it is necessary to name them if we want to understand and/or change the world. Those who commit acts of violence must be held accountable for their actions.

For example, it is O.K. for women to say that men have the vast majority of power in our society or for people of color to talk about the pervasiveness of white supremacy. It is O.K. for people in the Third World to challenge the First World nations' use of the majority of the world's resources. The discomfort caused by questioning these power relationships inevitably brings charges of "us-them" thinking or coercion, but it cannot be compared to the violence involved in enforcing those relationships.

Tactically, there are reasons to avoid alienating those who hold power. But this alienation can only be avoided if people "within the system" (or members of "oppressor groups") take some responsibility for continuing this dialogue.

3) Aren't you lumping together "legitimate" conservative political activity with hate groups such as Neo-Nazis?

No; we are not equating the two groups. Harassment and coercive political activity are quite different from non-coercive persuasion. But to limit our focus to extreme groups would assume that these groups are the sole champions of inequality: if they were to dissolve tomorrow, everything would suddenly get better. This is not the case. More mainstream conservative groups

Terry Laban/ In These Times

— whose audience is much larger — preach an ideology that assumes the "free market" can rectify social inequality. They fan the flames of hate and intolerance — the sources of violence — by scapegoating marginalized groups for society's ills. They advocate policies that cause more widespread social and economic devastation than extremist groups could inflict. Challenge racism and sexism no matter where they come from and what form they take.

4) Shouldn't professors be free to be spontaneous in class?

Of course. The problem occurs when professors' assumptions about the students in their classes get in the way of teaching. When they do not use inclusive language or are not respectful of the new perspectives brought by students of diverse backgrounds, they are not fully including these students in the educational process. Nor are they opening the classroom to truly critical thought, including the rethinking of "traditional" canons. Learning and open-mindedness apply not only to students, but teachers as well.

5) To be fair, shouldn't student activity boards refrain from funding political activities, or from funding "left" activities more than "right" ones?

Student fees were established at many schools so that student activities can be controlled democratically by students alone, and not be limited to those which support the policies of the university administration.

With or without funding from student fees, many student governments have enacted policies which forbid the use of student funds for "political activities." While the university's non-profit status justifies a ban on supporting partisan (i.e. Democratic or Republican) political campaigns, a ban on all student funding of political activities — as approved in 1993 by the California Supreme Court decision *Smith v. Regents* — is antidemocratic.

This policy plays into the strategy of the Right by forcing student groups to rely on funding external to the university. Such a policy is hardly "apolitical." It biases student expression to reflect the existing order, thus perpetuating the inequities of our society. In other words, students whose views coincide with the interests of corporations, wealthy individuals, or the Defense Establishment find it easy to obtain funds to express their views. But students with alternative viewpoints will be financially limited, even if their views are popular.

Tips on Responding to the Right Wing

by Rich Cowan

Success sometimes has a price. If your group wins a campaign, or is successful at getting its message across, you may be attacked by Right-wing forces on your campus.

If attacked you basically have three options. You can ignore the attacks, engage the attackers in a debate, or apply a sanction which will put an end to the attack. Keep in mind that an attack is not necessarily a bad thing. As in a game of chess, if your opponent's attack is weak you may wind up way ahead after the exchange. Instead of losing support, a progressive group can expose the history, tactics, and funding of the Right, turning this Right-wing disruption into an embarrassing scandal.

Sometimes the best course of action will be obvious; often not. The debate about what to do will be a contentious one, and has split many progressive groups. If we do not quickly mend these splits, we will fall into the traps set for us by the Right. This article offers a framework for discussion so that our groups can more quickly reach a consensus.

These guidelines may also help you respond to a sectarian-left group who attacks you for not following their "party line" closely enough.

In such discussions, it is important to evaluate whether the Right's provocations reflect a sincere desire to present an alternative point of view, or whether the agenda is primarily to disrupt your campaign. It is also very important to monitor the tide of student opinion: do not lose touch with your constituency.

A. Ignoring the attack

Many students today have a disdain for politics because they view it as a shouting match between two extreme points of view. Since the campus Right generally has money, not numbers, this situation works to their advantage by discouraging mass political involvement. At all costs, avoid mudslinging that merely puts a bad taste in people's mouths.

When the young Republicans publicly challenged a peace group I was in to a debate, we refused unless the student government would sponsor it. This sponsorship provided legitimacy to political debate and engaged new people on campus, rather than just preaching to the converted.

Sometimes an attack is so low that no response is necessary. Disclosing the nature of the attack alone will build sympathy to your cause even without discussion of the issues. If the attack is personal, try to have someone else respond other than the person attacked; an injury to one is an injury to all.

Often ignoring those on the offensive makes them all the more angered, leading them to engage in even more aggressive attacks, that are often incredibly unfounded.

B. Levels of engagement

The following are some possible ways to respond, from a minimal level of engagement to greater levels. In general, we recommend minimizing the engagement; if a Right-wing group has a tiny audience, you only increase that audience by engaging them. However, one or two people spreading misinformation in a systematic fashion may cause potential supporters to question your entire campaign. In this case, you will be better off if you are ready with a response. A few ideas:

- **Don't bring yourself down to their level.** A minimal level of engagement might be making a public statement as to why you do not intend to get into a harangue with the group. Perhaps you could shoot down just one of their arguments as an example of why you think students should not take the rest of their arguments seriously.

- **We know what you're against, but what are you for?** For example, many Right-wing groups question affirmative action. Granted, affirmative action laws do not result in perfect decisions. But do the conservatives have any constructive plan to rectify structural inequalities? Do they assert that these inequalities have been rectified?

- **Question the arguments directly.** If the Right is well-trained and reaches a large audience, your best defenses will be a good political line.   Keep in mind some vulnerabilities of the Right:

  1) The "Politically Correct" label is not as effective as it once was; it is now a "tired argument."

  2) The leftist campus climate that is often alleged by the Right simply does not exist; if you can demonstrate how Right-wing interests dominate your school's governance, people won't take the Right's charges seriously.

  3) The Right's arguments are often based on purely anecdotal evidence and bad science.

  4) The interests of students making $10,000 a year are really not the same as those of corporate sponsors of the Right, making

$400K per year.

- **Question their "Americanism."** Part of what makes the US attractive is the right of citizens to oppose their government. If the Right is so patriotic, why do they oppose our involvement in dissent? Remind people that McCarthyite tactics designed to ruin faculty careers and freedom of expression are hardly "American."

- **Question their independence.** Use this Guide to show how your local Right-wing group may not be an independent grass-roots group, but part of a top-down, nationally coordinated strat-egy. Ask the group whose training seminars they attend. Is there an obvious connection between their funding and the arguments they present? **(See "Tips on Challenging Outside Funding," p. 89.)**

- **"There is no defense against ridicule,"** wrote Saul Alinsky in *Rules for Radicals.* Ridiculing someone's arguments can be very effective — especially in those cases where the Right's arguments are, well, ridiculous.

C. The Free Speech/ Harassment/ Censorship Debate

The Right may deliberately operate in a gray zone between legitimate political activity and harassment. The best advice we can give to a group is to establish clear, justifiable definitions of disruption, harassment, intimidation, and hate literature in advance, and a process to take action when your political opponents cross that line. Free speech is not with-out limits; if your school fails to respond to harassment your group should organize a response.

For example, Right-wing campus newspapers sometimes print racist articles and then attack those who react as would-be censors. In 1995, at the University of Wisconsin/Milwaukee, the Latino Student Union got the chancellor to denounce the content of an article in the *UWM Times* — but not censor their right to publish. With this official denun-ciation, students were able to successfully challenge the university sub-sidy received by the paper in the form of office space.

Some administrations — particularly at Catholic colleges — may not be as supportive with attacks on gay, lesbian and bisexual organizations, who still do not enjoy constitutional protection against harassment.

All progressive groups that have succeeded over the long haul have established mechanisms to prevent disruption and infiltration by individ-uals, Right-wing or not. *The War at Home* by Brian Glick (South End Press) provides some excellent advice.

[Thanks to Ron Francis for discussions which improved this article.]

Suggestions for Engaging the Right

1) Do not focus on the "threat" they pose. You are on firmer ground when challenging their agenda.

2) Remember that this is a fight for control of the political mainstream.
- Avoid becoming a zealot and thus marginalizing yourself.
- Limit the emotionalism of your response.
- Ensure your credibility by researching your position, and don't misrepresent theirs.

3) If you criticize the Right for imposing their social views upon others, you are using politics in an appropriate way.
- Americans are fundamentally uneasy about having religious or social views imposed on them.

4) Engage in debates over specific issue positions rather than general values.
- Force them to defend their most extreme positions.
- When debating an issue, be sure you present a solution, rather than defending the status quo.
- Avoid getting positioned outside the mainstream on questions of core values.

5) Highlight the limited range of values advocated by the Right.
- Challenge their claim to speak for all religious Americans.
- Don't be afraid to expose how the Religious Right's claim of "values" is often a thin veil over the promotion of prejudice and bigotry.

6) Do not allow the Right to define political differences as a debate over the importance of religion or values.
- Don't allow them to accuse you of "Christian bashing."
- Don't allow them to define you as "anti-Christian."

7) It is critical to be on the offensive.
- Right-wing groups often gain prominence by attacking some-

thing or somebody. They are generally poor at defending themselves. So seize the initiative, and keep them on the defensive.
• Use their own words to attack them. Make them justify their
existence.

[Reprinted from the Freedom To Learn Network newsletter.]

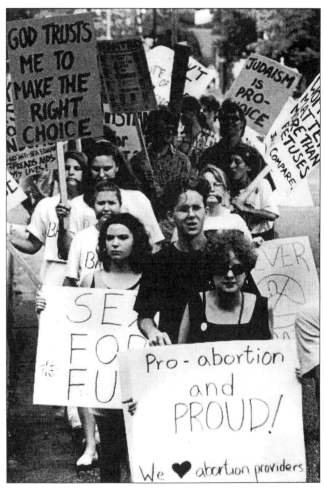

*Abortion Rights March, May 1992, Gainesville, Florida, photo
from Pete Self/ Gainesville Iguana*

Organization Research: Tracking the Flow of Funds

by Rich Cowan

Some organizations receive 80% or more of their funds from foundations listed in the *Foundation Grants Index*. Tracking the funding of these groups is easier than ever because the Foundation Center now publishes an annual called *Who Gets Grants; Who Gives Grants*. Each volume gives a concise list of foundation grants for thousands of organizations for one year.

Unfortunately, many conservative groups receive most of their funds from other sources, so additional investigation is often necessary. Here are some tips on tracking funding from these other sources:

1) The organization may receive money from foundations too small to be included in the *Foundation Grants Index*. In this case, you can still learn the amount of the grants if you know the names of the foundations, using their 990-PF forms (see box at right). The Foundation Center office in New York (tel. 212-620-4230) and Washington (tel. 202-331-1400) keep 990-PF forms for all US foundations.

2) The organization may receive large sums of money from corporations, family trusts, or wealthy individuals who are not required to disclose their contributions like a public foundation. These situations are difficult. If the group is tax-exempt, obtain its Form 990 tax return (see page 91) which may list larger donors. Also, many state attorney general's offices require non-profits to file disclosure forms before soliciting in that state. For-profit corporations are usually exempt from such disclosure laws.

3) The organization may receive funding from a government agency such as the DOD or the US Institute of Peace. You may need to file a Freedom of Information Act (FOIA) request to obtain a copy of the contract. The FOIA law will occasionally yield results in as little as two weeks. Military, intelligence and police agencies often have a year-long backlog and exempt some materials from release for reasons of "national security."

4) The organization may be a political action committee or partisan campaign committee. Federal disclosure laws require such committees to publish a report listing the names and home addresses of all donors giving over a certain amount, usually $50. Many states and towns also have strong disclosure laws. You cannot always tell how money is spent. For example, the Republican party collects tens of millions of dollars every year, but does not disclose how much goes to the Young Republicans.

A final word of advice: collect literature used by the group as you begin your search. Ask them to send information on their group and any publications they carry (using a pseudonym is recommended). See how much material you can get for free, and then scan it for lists of sponsors. Once you know the names of the sponsors, you may be able to contact them to obtain a grants list which lists the amounts donated.

drawing by Ben Leon

Foundation Research

by Sara Diamond

The *Foundation Grants Index* is published annually by the New York-based Foundation Center. It is available at most university libraries and larger public libraries. While not comprehensive, it very useful. Organized first by state and then by foundation, entries show dollar amounts and describe projects funded. It also contains indexes by foundation, grant recipient, and subject, and full addresses for all foundations.

Once you know the location(s) of the foundation(s) you're interested in, call or write to request an "annual report." Many foundations provide these free to inquirers. A well-produced annual report gives you itemized lists of grant recipients, dollar amounts, and brief project descriptions.

If a foundation does not produce an annual report or is unwilling to send it, grant listings are available through the Internal Revenue Service (IRS). All tax-exempt private foundations must file an annual "Form 990-PF" (PF stands for private foundation) tax return with the IRS. On this form, the foundation lists its assets, officers, and an itemized list of grantees. 990-PF forms are maintained at IRS regional service centers. The addresses and geographical boundaries of the centers change, so you should get current addresses from your local IRS office.

Once you know the address for the regional center covering the location of the foundation, write to that center and request "Form 990-PF." Give the name of the foundation, the address if possible, and the year that you're requesting. Filings for 1993 may not be available until 1994.

Some regional centers will send you a bill which you must pay before the materials are mailed. Others send Forms 990-PF right away, accompanied by an invoice. For a single year of a large foundation's filings, expect to pay at least $10.

To research organizations receiving corporate foundation money, start with the *Encyclopedia of Associations* and the *Research Centers Directory*. Both multi-volume sets are published by Gale Research, Inc. and available at university libraries.

[*Reprinted with permission from* Covert Action, *Fall 1991.*]

An Introduction to Propaganda Analysis

by Chip Berlet

The Right-wing publications now distributed on many campuses have the potential to create a great deal of political and journalistic confusion. In analyzing and in responding to the Right, it is useful to remember that academia has produced a long list of useful tools and techniques to evaluate the logical and conceptual validity of any argument regardless of political content or viewpoint.

Useful standards by which to judge the merits of any statement or theory are easily found in textbooks on debate, rhetoric, argument, and logic. These books discuss which techniques of argumentation are not valid because they fail to follow rules of logic. Among the more common fallacious techniques or inadequate proofs:

- Raising the volume, increasing the stridency, or stressing the emotionalism of an argument does not improve its validity. This is called argument by exhortation.

- Sequence does not imply causation. If Joan is elected to the board of directors of a bank on May 1, and Raul gets a loan on July 26, further evidence is needed to prove a direct or causal connection.

- Association does not imply agreement, hence the term "guilt by association" has a pejorative meaning. Association proves association: it suggests further questions are appropriate, and demonstrates the parameters of networks, coalitions, and personal moral distinctions — nothing more.

- Participation in an activity, or presence at an event, does not imply control.

- Congruence in one or more elements does not establish congruence in all elements. Gloria Steinem and Jeane Kirkpatrick are both intelligent, assertive women accomplished in political rhetoric. To assume they therefore also agree politically would be ludicrous. If milk is white and powdered chalk is white, would you drink a glass of powdered chalk?

- Similarity in activity does not imply joint activity and joint activity does not imply congruent motivation. When a person serves in an official advisory role or acts in a position of responsibility within a group, however, the burden of proof shifts to favor a presumption that such a person is not a mere member or associate, but probably embraces a considerable portion of the sentiments expressed by the group. Still, even members of boards of directors will distance themselves from a particular stance adopted by groups they oversee, and therefore it is not legitimate to assume automatically that they personally hold a view expressed by the group or other board members. It is legitimate, however, to assert that they need to distance themselves publicly from a particular organizational position if they wish to dissociate themselves from it.

- Anecdotes alone are not conclusive evidence. Anecdotes are used to illustrate a thesis, not to prove it.

- Lack of evidence is not proof, nor even a suggestion, of a possible conspiracy. Just because an incident lacks an apparently obvious explanation, or a person fails to do something that seems obviously required or effective, it doesn't imply a sinister motive or plot.

In 1936 Boston merchant Edward Filene helped establish the short-lived Institute for Propaganda Analysis which sought to educate Americans to recognize propaganda techniques. Alfred McClung Lee, Institute director from 1940-2, and his wife Elizabeth Briant Lee, co-authors of *The Fine Art of Propaganda, Social Problems in America,* recently wrote an article in the periodical Propaganda Review which they suggested that educating the public about propaganda techniques was an urgent priority.

The Lees developed a list of seven hallmark tricks of the manipulative propagandist:

Name Calling: hanging a bad label on an idea
Card Stacking: selective use of facts or outright falsehoods
BandWagon: a claim that everyone like us thinks this way
Testimonial: the association of a respected or hated person with an idea
Plain Folks: a technique whereby the idea and its proponents are linked to "people like you and me"
Transfer: an assertion of a connection between something valued or hated and the idea or commodity being discussed
Glittering Generality: an association of something with a "virtue word" to gain approval without examining the evidence

[Excerpted from "Right Woos Left," a paper published by Political Research Associates, Cambridge, MA, in 1993.]

Tips on Challenging Outside Funding

by Rich Cowan

If Right-wing organizations receiving thousands of dollars in outside grants are operating at your campus, try the following to encourage constructive discussion about the impact of this funding:

A. Use this guide to begin examining the funding of these groups. Contact CCO if you need assistance.

B. Write about the influence of right-wing funding on campus. Point out the imbalance in funding for groups which support the interests of those who have power vs. the interest of groups which work for the disenfranchised.

C. See if your student activities funding board has a policy on funding groups that maintain outside affiliations to national organizations. Such policies are common at many universities. We do not oppose ties to national organizations; but we think that these ties should be disclosed to prevent wealthy groups from covertly purchasing the allegiance of students. The same principle was cited to win passage of campaign reform laws, which require disclosure of larger contributions and put a ceiling on the maximum gift. You could advocate a disclosure policy containing the following:

   1) disclosure of ties (affiliate status) to outside organizations,
   2) disclosure of financial support, not including sale of goods or ad space, from outside organizations,
   3) a procedure for members of the campus community to inspect the disclosure forms,
   4) penalties for failure to honestly disclose, and
   5) guidelines that reduce allocations given to groups which receive outside support from student activities fees

D. If you succeed in enacting such a disclosure policy, you can counter the corporations who fund the Right at your campus by organizing boycotts, counter-recruitment campaigns, etc.

Expose the Administration:
Researching Your Campus Power Structure

by Rich Cowan and Nicole Newton

Right-wing activity on campus is not limited to outside pressure groups; it is often present within your own university's administration and board of trustees. University administrators use a standard bag of excuses to resist calls for democratic reform, such as the claim that they can't find "qualified" minority faculty members and that ethnic studies requirements create "bias" in the curriculum. To avoid "politicizing" discussion, administrators rarely open meetings to students. Many university technocrats believe that if we wait forty years, sexism and racism will disappear. Others believe it already has.

Successful organizing always depends on knowing who pulls the strings and directs the flow of money, and research is necessary to reveal your university's connections to special interests. You should know how much funding comes from tuition, the state, the federal government, corporate research and user fees, alumni contributions, and student fees. A careful examination of your Board of Trustees is a quick way to evaluate special interest control within your university.

The well-tested research techniques presented below were used by students at the University of Massachusetts, MIT, Rutgers, and the University of Texas at Austin.

1) Compile General Information

In early September, the *Chronicle of Higher Education* releases its annual "Almanac issue" containing statistical tables from past year publications which are sorted by university. Acquire three university documents from the local library: the annual treasurer's report, the annual report on sponsored research, and the annual reports of various department heads to the president. If the library does not have public copies of these documents, request copies from the appropriate university offices.

2) Research Administration Salaries

Private universities must file IRS tax form 990, which requires a list of the top ten officials' salaries. Sine 1988, all non-profit organizations are supposed to make this form available for public inspection during regular business hours. In some states, these reports are kept on file in the public charities division of the state attorney general's office. You can also call 1–800-TAX-FORM and request form 4506-A from the Internal Revenue Service, "Request for Public Inspection or Copy of Exempt Organization Tax Form." The president of Boston University made over $350,000 in 1994; the average college president salary was over $110,000. Top administrative salaries at public universities are in the state budget. The regents and president are required to file financial disclosure with the state. Check with the same bureaucracy that handles financial disclosures for political candidates, or call the president's or regents' offices and ask for a copy.

7) Investigate University Budget Priorities

Try obtaining budget information from student trustees, sympathetic faculty, department chairpersons, and the provost's office. At private universities, some budget information is contained in Form 990. At public universities, the Freedom of Information Act or Sunshine Law of your state may give complete access. The Secretary of State's office in your state has listings of university-owned trusts, affiliated investment corporations, and university bond filings for construction projects. You can even get a copy of your school's bylaws, which may include ignored democratic procedures.

8) Find Major University Donors

Major gifts and grants to the university should be listed in university's complete treasurer's report. IRS 990 forms may list all donors of more than $5000 to your school, with addresses. Try to get this information directly from the portion of the campus bureaucracy which solicits donations. Find the top bureaucrat and request a listing. At public universities, donor lists should be a matter of public record. At the first sign of resistance file an open records request for the information.

9) Locate University Portfolios and Corporate Connections

A full treasurer's report will usually list investments. Since these investments also change, you will want to request a more current list as Tufts students did before waging a divestment campaign.

10) Investigate Tuition and Financial Aid vs. Inflation

Back issues of any large U.S. almanac such as the "World Almanac" list thousands of college tuition figures for a given year. Try the Statistical Abstract of the US for additional statistics. The university financial aid office should provide financial aid statistics to you.

11) Track Minority Enrollment and Faculty Representation

Your university is required to keep enrollment statistics if it accepts government funds. A summary by race appears each year in the *Chronicle of Higher Education* for all colleges except those which escape the reporting requirement by refusing government money (i.e. Hillsdale College). Network with minority student representatives to see if these figures are correct.

Request a tally of minority and women faculty by department and by tenure status from the President or Provost of your school. If affirmative action is endorsed by the administration but left up to individual departments, are they ignoring this policy? Publicize the numbers so departments with bad records will feel the heat and open up positions to untenured women or faculty of color.

12) Investigate Sexual and Racial Harassment

You are likely to encounter obstacles when digging for this information. Check campus police crime reports, but remember internal university records on harassment by faculty members are seldom disclosed.

It may be helpful to consult the discrimination related government agencies of your city and state, the US Department of Education, and the Equal Employment Opportunity Commission (EEOC). Finally, go to the clerk's office in the courthouse of the county in which your school is located to see if your school is a defendant in any active cases which may relate to sex or race discrimination. Look up the docket numbers of the cases involving your university and request to see them.

13) Research, Science, and Education Statistics

Call the National Science Board (an arm of the National Science Foundation) at (703) 306-1234 for a copy of *Science Indicators,* which is published every two years. If you tell them the copy is for a review by your campus newspaper, they'll probably send you the 400-page book free!

14) Research Government and Military Contracts

Your university sponsored "research" office may provide you with a free listing of all externally funded research, both corporate and military. If they do not, remind them that as a taxpayer you have a right to information on publicly funded research!

RESOURCES FOR

FIGHTING THE RIGHT

Suggested Reading List

Key Publications from the Right Wing

Anderson, Martin. *Imposters in the Temple.* New York: Simon and Schuster, 1992.

Bennett, William. *To Reclaim a Legacy: A Report on the Humanities in Higher Education.* Washington, DC: National Endowment for the Humanities, 1984.

Bernstein, David, ed. *Diversity and Division: A Critical Journal of Race and Culture* (serial). Madison Center for Educational Affairs.

Bloom, Alan. *Closing of the American Mind..* New York: Simon and Schuster, 1987.

D'Souza, Dinesh. *Illiberal Education.* New York: Harper & Row, 1990.

D'Souza, Dinesh. *The End of Racism: Principles for a Multiracial Society.* New York: The Free Press, , 1995, p. 527.

Kimball, Roger. *Tenured Radicals.* New York: Harper & Row. 1990.

Simon, William. *A Time for Truth.* New York: Readers Digest Press. 1987.

Steele, Shelby. *The Content of Our Character.* New York: St. Martin Press. 1992.

Sykes, Charles J. *PROFSCAM: Professors and the Demise of Higher Education.* Washington: Regnery Gateway, Inc., 1988.

Background on the Right Wing

Bellant, Russ. *Old Nazis, the New Right, and the Republican Party.* South End Press, 1989.

Berlet, Chip, ed., *Eyes Right! Challenging the Right-wing Backlash,* South End Press, Boston, MA, 1995.

Clarkson, Fred. "Reagan Youth: The War of Ideas," *Interchange Report* Winter/Spring 1985.

Economics America, Inc. *The Right Guide,* Fourth Edition. Ann Arbor: Economics America, Inc. 1997.

Faludi, Susan. *Backlash.* New York: Crown Publishers, 1991. A definitive book on antifeminism.

Wolf, Louis. "Accuracy in Media Rewrites the News and History." *Covert Action.* 21 Spring 1984, pp. 24-29.

Affirmative Action

Ayres, B. Drummond, "Foes of Affirmative Action Form Group to Spread Message," *New York Times*, January 16, 1997.

Jascik, Scott, "Affirmative Action under Fire," *The Chronicle of Higher Education,* March 10, 1995.

Free Speech and Hate Crimes

American Association of State Colleges and Universities, "*How the First Amendment Applies to Offensive Expression on the Campuses of Public Colleges and Universities,*" and "*Academic Freedom and 'Political Correctness,*" (pamphlets).

Anti-Defamation League. *Combatting Bigotry on Campus.* New York: 1989. Describes both spontaneous hate crimes and public acts of "organized bigotry" on campus.

Delgado, Richard and Jean Stefancic. "Overcoming Legal Barriers to Regulating Hate Speech on Campuses," *The Chronicle of Higher Education,* August 11, 1993, pp. B1-B4.

Hively, Robert, Ed. *The Lurking Evil: Racial and Ethnic Conflict on the College Campus.* Washington: American Association of State Colleges and Universities, 1990.

Keeble, John, "The Southern League: Waving the Confederate Battle Flag, a Growing Group of Deep South Academics Argues for a White Nationalism They Call Cracker Culture," *Village Voice*, June 11, 1996.

Wilson, Robin. "New White-Student Unions on Some Campuses Are Sparking Outrage and Worry," *The Chronicle of Higher Education*, April 18, 1990, p. A1.

PC Debates

Aufderhide, Patricia, Ed. *Beyond P.C. Toward a Politics of Understanding.* St. Paul: Graywolf Press, 1992.

Beers, David. "P.C? B.S.: Behind the Hysteria," *Mother Jones*, Sept/Oct 1991.

Cockburn, Alexander. "Bush and P.C.— A Conspiracy So Immense..." *The Nation*, May 27, 1991. pp. 687, 690-691, 704.

Faludi, Susan, "I'm not a Feminist but I Play one on TV," *Ms.*, March April, 1995, p. 31.

Raskin, Jamin. "The Fallacies of Political Correctness," *Z Magazine.* Jan 1992. Examines myths about "political correctness" and common flaws in analyzing censorship.

Wilson, John K., *The Myth of Political Correctness: The Conservative Attack on Higher Education.* Durham: Duke University Press, 1995.

Curricular Change/Academic Freedom

Brodkey, Linda. "Transvaluing Difference." *College English*. Oct. 1989.

Diamond, Sara. "Readin', Writin', and Repressin.'" *Z Magazine*. Feb 1991.

Duster, Troy. "They're Taking Over! and Other Myths about Race on Campus." *Mother Jones*, Sept/Oct 1991.

Glazer, Myron and Glazer. *Whistle Blowers*. New York: Basic Books. Looks at what happens to professors who speak up about discrimination in the academy.

Messer-Davidow, Ellen. "Manufacturing the Attack on Liberalized Higher Education." *Social Text*. Summer 1993, p.40-80.

Rothenberg, Paula. "Critics of Attempts to Democratize the Curriculum..." *Chronicle of Higher Education*. April 10, 1991.

Soley, Lawrence C., *Leasing the Ivory Tower*, South End Press, 1995.

Stedt, Margaret, "Curricular Change: Still Under Fire at Georgetown University," from a forthcoming issue of the newsletter of the National Association for Women in Catholic Higher Education, Spring 1997.

Trask, Haunani-Kay. "Firing of Progressive Professors: The Politics of Academic Freedom vs. the Politics of White Racism." *From a Native Daughter*. Monroe, Maine: Common Courage Press, 1993.

Weisberg, Jacob. "NAS: Who Are These Guys Anyway?" *Lingua Franca*, April 1991.

Wiener, John. "Campus Voices Right and Left" *The Nation*. December 12, 1988.

Williams, Patricia J., "Blockbusting the Canon." *Ms*. Sept.-Oct. 1991. An African-American law professor at the Univ. of Wisconsin looks at the PC war on campus, in her classes, and against her.

Funding

Bellant, Russ. *The Coors Connectio: How Coors Family Philanthropy Undermines Democratic Pluralism*. Cambridge MA: Political Research Associates, April 1990. Analyzes a network of ultra-conservative institutions financed by Coors affecting many progressive movements.

Bleifuss, Joel, "Doing Right by the Campus Left," *In These Times*, Jan. 22, 1996

Cowan, Rich, "Developing a Youth Strategy: Lessons from the Right," in *Responsive Philanthrophy*, Newsletter of the Nat'l Comm. for Responsive Philanthropy, Spring 1997.

Egen, Rachel, "Buying a Movement: Right-Wing Foundations and American Politics," Washington, DC: People for the American Way, 1996.

Greene, Stephen and Jennifer Moore, " Conservative Foundations on the Move," *The Chronicle of Philanthropy,* February 23, 1995.

Kuntz, Phil, "Citizen Scaife: Heir Turned Publisher Uses Financial Largess to Fuel Conservatism," *Wall Street Journal*, 10/12/95 p. A5.

Mundy, Liza. "The Dirty Dozen: Academia's Skankiest Funder." *Lingua Franca*. March/April, 1993, pp. 1, 24-31.

Messer-Davidow, Ellen "Who (Ac)Counts and How." *MMLA Journal* 27, 1 (Spring 1994): 26-41.

Messer-Davidow, Ellen, "Dollars for Scholars: The Real Politics of Humanities Scholarship and Programs," *The Politics of Research*, ed. E. Ann Kaplan and George Levine (New Brunswick: Rutgers UP, 1997).

Miner, Barbara, "The Power and the Money: Bradley Foundation Bankrolls Conservative Agenda," *Rethinking Schools*, Spring 1994, Vol. 8, No. 3.

Rothmayer, Karen. "The Mystery Angel of the New Right," *The Washington Post*. July 12, 1981. pp. C1, C4.

Rothmeyer, Karen. "Citizen Scaife." *Columbia Journalism Review*. July/August, 1981, pp. 41-50.

Rothmeyer, Karen. "Scaife's Seed Money Helps New Right Blossom." *Common Cause*. August, 1981.

Saloma, John S. III. *Ominous Politics: New Conservative Labyrinth*. New York: Hill & Wang Pub, 1984. Explains the self-perpetuating funding net of the Right.

Stefanic, Jean and Richard Delgado, *No Mercy: How conservative Think Tanks and Foundations Changed America's Social Agenda,* Temple University Press, 1997.

Warner, David. "Scaife: Financier of the Right," *Pittsburgh Post-Gazette*. April 20, 1981.

Wiener, Jon. "Money for Neo-Conservative Scholars." *The Nation*. Jan 1, 1990.

Religious Right/Anti-choice

Bloedow, Jonathan, "God and Journalism on Campus," *World*, April 4, 1995.

"Christian Coalition Expands Its Agenda," *Human Events*. Nov. 6,1993.

Clarkson, Frederick and Skipp Porteous. *Challenging the Christian Right: The Activist's Handbook*. Institute for First American Studies, Inc. PO Box 589, Great Barrington, MA 01230 (413) 274-3786.

Diamond, Sara. *Spiritual Warfare*. South End Press, 1989.

Southern Educational Communications. Firing Line Debate. *"Resolved: We need not fear the Christian Right"* Video #114. Aired by PBS, 1993. 2700 Cypress St Columbia, SC 29205. (803) 799-3449.

Campus Newspapers

Bloedow, Jonathan, " God and Journalism pn Campus," World, April, 1 1995, p 12

Schulman, Beth, "Foundations for a Movement: How the Right Wing Subsidizes its Press," *EXTRA!*, March/April 95, p. 12

Seligman, Miles and Cymbre Simpson. "Behind Right-Wing Campus Newspapers," *Extra!*, Sept/Oct 1991, p. 9.

Smith, Jeremy, Students, "Faculty and Political Engagment" *Social Text*, Summer 1997

Pro-militarism

"The Cold Warriors." *Common Cause Magazine.* July/August, 1985.

Desruisseaux, Paul. "Expanding International Study." *The Chronicle of Higher Education.* Nov. 24, 1993, pp. A34-35. Detailed look at the National Security Education Act.

Landis, Fred. "*CIA Psychological Warfare Operations in Nicaragua, Chile and Jamaica,*" Science for the People. Jan/Feb 1982.

Relyea, Harold C. "The American Security Council." *The Nation.* January 24, 1972, pp. 113-16.

Other Bibliographies

Nordquist, Joan, Compiler. *The Multicultural Education Debate in the University: A Bibliography*. Santa Cruz, CA: Reference and Research Services. 1992. Number 25 in the Contemporary Social Issues series.

Political Research Associates. Extensive bibliographies on "Political Correctness" & Multiculturalism; Conservatism and the Electoral Right Wing; Race, Ethnicity, Religion & Culture; Gender, Sexuality & Sexual Preference; Authoritarianism, Fascism, Nazism & Totalitarianism; Homophobia & the Religious & Political Right; the Holocaust; Political Repression; Wise Use/Property Rights Movement; and various individuals with histories of Right-wing involvement.

HELPFUL ORGANIZATIONS

compiled by the CCO Staff

American-Arab Anti-Discrimination Committee — 4201 Connecticut Ave, NW, Suite 300, Washington, DC 20008, (202) 244-2990. Independent organization defending the rights of and promoting the heritage of Arab-Americans. adc@adc.org

Americans United for the Separation of Church and State — 1816 Jefferson Pl NW, Washington, DC 20036, (202)466-3234. An organization supporting litigation in support of the separation between church and state.

Anti-Defamation League of B'nai B'rith — 823 UN Plaza, New York, NY 10017, (212) 490-2525. Extensive resources on many white supremacist and Christian Right groups. Note: ADL has been criticized for sharing information on Arab activists with government agencies.

Associations of scholars in ethnic and women's studies — African Studies Association; Asian/American Center; Association for the Study of Afro-American Life and History; Association of Asian Studies; Association of Caribbean Studies; Center for Studies of Ethnicity and Race in America; Chicana/Latina Research Project; Coalition for Western Women's History; Conference Group on Women's History; Cross-Cultural Black Women's Studies Summer Institute; Inter-University Program for Latino Research; Latin American Studies Association; National Association for Black Studies; National Association for Chicano Studies; National Association for Ethnic Studies; National Women's Studies Association; Puerto Rican Studies Association; Sociologists for Women in Society

Bay Area Coalition for our Reproductive Rights — 750 La Playa Suite 730, San Francisco, CA 94121, (415)437-4032. Publishes amazingly detailed research reports linking anti-abortion and white supremacist groups. tburghardt@igc.apc.org

Campus Violence Prevention Center — Towson State U, Towson, MD 21204, (410) 830-2178. Produces publications and holds conferences on campus ethnoviolence and how it can be addressed.

Center for Democratic Renewal — PO Box 50469, Atlanta, GA 30302, (404) 221-0025. Monitors white supremacist activity; also addressses issues of campus violence.

Center for Women Policy Studies — 1211 Conneticut Ave.NW, NW, Suite 312, Washington, DC 20036, (202) 872-1770. Among other programs, runs a project entitled *Violence Against Women as Gender Bias-motivated Hate Crime*, including two policy papers on the issue.

Committee Against Anti-Asian Violence — 191 E 3rd St, New York, NY 10009, (212) 473-6485. Publishes a newsletter. caaav@dti.net

DC Student Coalition Against Racism — P.O Box 18291, Washington, DC 20036, (212) 310-2930. Ten-year-old organization dedicated to action and education in battling racism in the U.S. and abroad. Dcscar@igc.apc.org

Fairness and Accuracy in Reporting — 130 W 25th St, New York, NY 10001, (212) 633-6700. Publishes the magazine *EXTRA!* of investigative reports; monitors right-wing bias in the news media. fair@fair.org

The Fund for the Feminist Majority - 1600 Wilson Blvd, Suite 801 Arlington, VA 22209. (703) 522-2214. Conducts research on anti-feminist hate groups and efforts to defeat affirmative action. femmaj@feminist.org

Holocaust Survivors & Friends in Pursuit of Justice — 800 New Loudon Rd, Suite 400, Latham, NY 12110, (518) 785-0035. Publishes materials refuting Holocaust deniers and Historical Revisionists.

Institute for First Amendment Studies, Inc.— P.O. Box 589, Great Barrington, MA 01230, (413) 528-3800. Publishes activist's handbook on "Challenging the Christian Right."

Interfaith Alliance - 1511 K Street, NW, Suite 738, Washington, DC, 20005, (202) 639-6370. A church and synagogue based organization that counters the religious right. TIAlliance@intr.net

National Abortion Federation — 1755 Mass Ave, NW, Washington, DC 20036; (202) 667-5881. Among other programs, collects information on anti-choice activities on campus.

National Council for Research on Women — 530 Broadway at Spring St, 10th floor, New York, NY 10012, (212) 274-0730. A working alliance of centers and organizations that provide resources for feminist research, policy analysis and educational programs.

National Gay and Lesbian Task Force — 2320 17th St. NW, Washington, DC 20009, 202-332-6483. Publishes 300-page guide for lesbigay student groups, and maintains a Fight The Right campaign to counter the assault on gay and lesbian communities. ngltf@ngltf.org

National Education Association Center for Advancement of Public Education — 1201 16th St. NW, Washington, DC 20036,

(202) 822-7446. New center established by NEA to counter Right-wing assault on public education.

OPENMIND, The Association for the Achievement of Cultural Diversity in Higher Education — Dept. of Materials Science & Engineering, SUNY at Stony Brook, Stony Brook, NY 11794-2275, (516) 632-8499. Seeks to increase cultural diversity among researchers and educators and to broaden the canon of knowledge and scholarship.

Oxfam America — 26 West St, Boston, MA 02111, (617) 482-1211. Independent international development organization that involves students in hunger issues and has been attacked by the Right.

People Against Racist Terror — PO Box 1055, Culver City, CA 90232, (310) 288-5003. Provides information on police brutality, racism, white supremacy, anti-Jewish and anti-Arab activity, fascism. Publishes "Turning the Tide: Journal of anti-racist activism, research and education." mnovickttt@igc.org

People for The American Way — 2000 M St NW, Suite 400, Washington, DC 20036, (202) 467-4999; fax: (202) 293-2672. Monitors all aspects of the Right, and has a project monitoring attacks on gays and lesbians in the U.S. pfaw@pfaw.org

Political Research Associates — 120 Beacon St., #202, Somerville, MA 02142, (617) 661-9313. Research institute on Right-wing organizations and activities nationwide, including those on campuses. The insitute houses extensive written materials, as well as provides reports, publications, bibliographies, speakers and classes. publiceye@igc.apc.org

Project Tocsin — P.O. Box 163523, Sacramento, CA 95816-3523, (916) 374-8726. Monitors religious right groups such as the Traditional Values Coalition.

SpeakOut! — c/o Institute for Social & Cultural Change, P.O. Box 99096, Emeryville, CA 94662. The nation's only not-for-profit progressivespeakers and artists agency. speakout@igc.apc.org

Teachers for a Democratic Culture — PO Box 6405, Evanston, IL 60204, (773) 955-2047. Association of academics who look at the misleading charge of "political correctness." Publishes a newsletter and organizes professors across the country. jkw3@amber.uchicago.edu

U.S. Public Interest Research Groups — 218 D St. SE, Washington, DC 20003, (202) 546-9707. Works with students nationwide on issues of social concern; has established a project on preserving student fee autonomy in the face of right-wing attacks. pirg@pirg.org

U.S. Student Association (USSA) — 1413 K St. NW, 10th Floor, Washington, DC 20005, (202) 347-8772. National association of student governments, working for students' interests. ussa@essential.org

Web Resources

Consult the CCO Web Link Page, wwo.cco.org/links, for a list of right-wing monitoring web resources.

How to reach publications listed in article credits:

Freedom to Learn Network - 202 Downeyflake Ln, Suite 301A, Allentown, PA 18103, (610) 838-2254

National Student News Service - 116 New Montgomery St. Suite 530, San Francisco, CA 9410, (415) 543-2089, fax (415) 543-1480, email nsns@igc.apc.org

Responsive Philanthropy - 2001 S St. NW, Suite 620, Washington, DC 20009, (202) 387-9177, $25/yr.

Village Voice-36 Cooper Square, New York, NY 10003, (212) 475-3300

Z Magazine - 11 Millfield Rd., Woods Hole, MA 02543, (508) 548-9063

APPENDICES

OTHER INFORMATION, GRAPHS, TABLES, AND DOCUMENTS

J. Klossner

Index of Right-Leaning Groups Operating on Campus

Accuracy in Academia — see article beginning on p. 31

Acton Institute — Religious group; holds weekend sessions training students in "Liberty," "Justice," and "Environmentalism"

American Academy for Liberal Education — New Right-wing college accrediting group

American Cause Foundation — Pat Buchanan's new group, dedicated to "Winning the Culture War"

Aryan Youth Movement — Promotes "White Student Unions"

Association of American Universities — Elite assoc. of research universities; supports military research

Association of Professional Schools of International Affairs — Elite assoc. of foreign policy schools; supports CIA funding

Campus Crusade for Christ — Huge campus membership; strong supporter of Ronald Reagan

CATO Institute — Primary Libertarian think tank

Center for Individual Rights — Provides free legal aid for those accused of sexism, racism, homophobia.

Center for Study of Popular Culture (pub. Heterodoxy) — see article beginning on p. 31

Charles Edison Memorial Youth Fund — Funds interns and trains students in free-market ideas

Citizens for the Environment — Corporate-funded group seeks "market-oriented solutions to environmental problems"

Coll. Republican Nat'l Comm — see article beginning on p. 31

Collegians Activated to Liberate Life — see article beginning on p. 31

Collegiate Assn. for the Research of Principles — Student chapters assoc. with Unification Church

Committee for a Constructive Tomorrow — Affiliated with the Wise-Use Movement

Concerned Women for America — Conservative women's reaction to National Organization for Women

Eagle Forum Collegians — Phyllis Schafly's antifeminist spinoff group agitates for family values & strong military

Educational & Research Institute — see article beginning on p. 31

Executive Intelligence Review — Publication of LaRouche organization

False Memory Syndrome Foundation — Charges that many memories of sexual abuse are imagined

Feminists for Life — Anti-abortion group

Fallout, the Leading Voice in Student Radio — Radio Project of USA Foundation (see below)

Federalist Society — Network of conservative law student organizations.

First Amendment Coalition — New national organization forming chapters at Ivy League schools; claims to be a "centrist" group

Fund for American Studies — Sponsors summer institutes at Georgetown for 200 students each summer

Free Congress Foundation — Key "New Right" group founded in 1974 by Adolph Coors and Paul Weyrich

Foundation for Economic Education — Battles against socialism in the tradition of Ludwig von Mises; holds student seminars

Heritage Foundation — Conservative think tank with $25 million budget, professors serving as "adjunct scholars"

Heterodoxy — see Center for the Study of Popular Culture

Hoover Institution — Right-wing think tank at Stanford University; promoted Reagan policies

Individual Rights Foundation — Protects offensive expression; helps fraternities charged with harrassment

Institute for Contemporary Studies — Distributes a catalog of conservative books and literature

Institute for Historical Review — Challenges whether the Holocaust actually occurred; places ads in student newspapers; active on computer networks

Institute for Humane Studies — Runs classes on "individual rights, free trade, peace, the rule of law, the free market, personal liberty"

Institute in Basic Youth Conflicts — Runs seminars on how to "be alert to spiritual danger and be a man"

Intercollegiate Studies Institute — see article beginning on p. 31

Institute for Objectivist Studies — Promotes objectivism, the individualist and "ultra-capitalist" philosophy of Ayn Rand

Int'l Society for Individual Liberty — Promotes "campus libertarian organizations" & "competitive economic systems"

Koch Foundation Fellowships — Pays students to study "individual liberty" and "private property" for 10 weeks in the summer

Leadership Institute — see article beginning on p. 31

Lincoln Institute for Public Policy Research — UltraRight African-American group; opposes African National Congress in South Africa

Ludwig Von Mises Institute — Auburn U Right-wing think-tank

Madison Center for Educational Affairs — Merged with ISI in 1995

National Alliance — Racist group, posts flyers to recruit on campus

National Association for the Advancement of White People — David Duke's organization

National Association of Scholars (pub. Academic Questions) — see article beginning on p. 31

National Empowerment Television — TV network founded in 1993 by the New Right; includes student programming

National Journalism Center — a project of Education and Research Institute.

National Traditionalist Caucus — Opposes taxes and gays; starts "support groups for straight kids." Junior high and high school focused

Pink Sheet on the Left — Virulent anti-communist newsletter on pink paper; works closely with College Republicans

Pioneer Fund — Sponsors eugenics research on genetic differences between whites and blacks

Political Economy Research Center — Montana State U pro-business, anti-environmental think tank

Public Education Coalition — Works against funding of public education

Reason Foundation — Libertarian think tank; publishes *Reason* magazine

Students for a Better America — Conservative group which disrupted CISPES in the 1980s

Students for America — Student group dedicated to preserving values God and Country, once directed by Ralph Reed

Students in Free Enterprise — Claimed 80 chapters of student free-market advocates

Third Millenium — see article beginning on p. 31

United States Industrial Council Ed. Foundation — Used to train journalists prior to Madison Center

University Faculty for Life — Faculty anti-abortion group centered at Georgetown U

University Professors for Academic Order — "Old Guard" professors group formed in reaction to Vietnam War protests

USA (United Students of America) Foundation — Non-profit arm of College Republicans

Western Goals Foundation — Anti-communist organization collects data files on left-wing activists

White Student Union — see Aryan Youth Movement

Women's Freedom Network — New organization opposing feminists under the guise of feminism

Young America's Foundation — see article beginning on p. 31

Young Americans for Freedom — membership organization of

Youth for Christ — Christian group which receives Right-wing funding

Right-Wing Universities

Christendom College (right-to-life)
Grove City College (PA, refused to not discriminate against women)
Hillsdale College (Michigan, totally pro-corporate and privately funded)
Independent University (right wing university in DC)
Liberty University
National Defense University
Regent University (Pat Robertson)

Anti-Public Interest Law Organizations

Landmark Legal Foundation
Mountain States Legal Foundation
New England Legal Foundation
Pacific Legal Foundation
Southeastern Legal Foundation
Washington Legal Foundation
Western Legal Foundation

KEY FUNDERS OF THE CAMPUS RIGHT, 1994-5

Foundation Name & State	Assets ($000,000)	Campus Grants ($000)	Source of Funds
Allegheny Fdn (PA)	26	375	Richard Mellon Scaife, son of Sarah Scaife (Gulf Oil Wealth)
Lynde & Harry Bradley Fdn (WI)	393	1106	Donors- Allen Bradley Corp., Harry L., Caroline D., Margaret B.
Carthage Fdn (PA)	12	195	Donated and controlled by Richard Mellon Scaife, son of Sarah Scaife
Castle Rock Fdn (CO)	41	225	Donor- Adolph Coors Foundation; Trustee William K. Coors
Communities Foundation of TX	246	20	
Cooper Industries Fdn (TX)	769	10	Cooper Industries, Inc.
Richard and Helen DeVos Fdn (MI)	134	85	Amway Corporation, living
William H. Donner (NY)	66	335	Pres. of Donner Steel Co., Inc., 1916-29
Earhart Fdn (MI)	56	87	Harry Boyd earhart, Pres., and Chairman of the Board, White Star Refining
William Stamps Farish Fund (TX)	88	10	William Stamps Farish, Pres., Standard Oil of NJ, 1933-7
Grover Hermann Fdn (CA)	61	45	Grover M. Hermann
Henry Salvatori Fdn (CA)	4	455	CA Oilman, backer of Ronald Reagan
Homeland Fdn (NY)	77	10	Chauncey Stillman, philantropist, 1907-1989, Harvard Grad
Jaquelin Hume Fdn (CA)	20	188	Jaqueline H. Hume, Caroline H. Hume, William J. Hume
JM Foundation (NY)	20	20	Jeremiah Milbank, Int'l Minerals and Chemical Corp., finance chair of Repub. Nat'l Cmte. during Hoover Admin.
F. M. Kirby Fdn (NY)	259	200	Donor- Kirby Family, F.M., Allan P.
Lilly Endowment Inc. (IN)	3,094	150	Family of Eli Lilly, Eli Lilly Inc. from 1923-1966
Montgomery Street Fdn (CA)	23	10	Crown Zellerbach Corp. purchased by James River Corp in 1986
MJ Murdock Charitable Trust (WA)	262	55	Donor- Melvin Jack Murdock
Samuel Roberts Noble Fdn (OK)	557	10	Samuel Roberts Noble
John M. Olin Fdn (NY)	151	870	Associated with Olin Corp., 1913-1982, Winchester Corp. (guns)
Smith Richardson Fdn (CT)	361	205	H. Smith Richardson, president, Vicks Chemical Corp (Vaporub), 1919-1929
Sarah Scaife Fdn (PA)	203	1825	Sarah Mellon Scaife (Gulf Oil Wealth)
Scaife Family Fdn (PA)	110	325	Richard Mellon Scaife, son of Sarah Scaife (Gulf Oil Wealth)
Barre Seid Fdn (IL)	8	35	Donor- Barre Seid
Stranahan Fdn	3	75	Robert A Stranahan, Pres. and chmn, Champion Spark Club Co., 1910-1962

[Note: "Campus Grants" are total of grants to 13 campus organizations listed on page 34, as reported in Who Gets Grants, Who Gives Grants, 1994-5. Research by Harley Gambill and Rich Cowan.]

The "Collegiate Network" Exposed:

Conservative Campus Newspapers Affiliated with the Madison Center for Educational Affairs

Brandeis U	The Brandeisian
Cornell U .	The Cornell Review
Dartmouth College	The Dartmouth Review
Duke U	The Duke Review
Florida State U	The Independent Perspective
Georgetown U .	The Academy
Harvard U	The Harvard Salient
Harvard U	The Peninsula
Johns Hopkins U	The Homewood Spectator
Kenyon College	The Kenyon Observer
Miami U	The Miami Review
MIT	Counterpoint★
North Carolina State U	The State Critic
Northwestern U	Northwestern Chronicle
Notre Dame	Dialogue at Notre Dame
Oberlin College	The Oberlin Forum
Pennsylvania State U	The Lionhearted
Princeton U	The Princeton Sentinel
Princeton U	The Princeton Tory
Rice U	The Rice Sentinel
Southern Illinois U	The Orange & Blue Observer★
Southern Methodist U	The University Standard★
Stanford U	The Stanford Review
SUNY Binghamton	The Binghamton Review
Texas Christian U	The University Standard★
Trinity College	The Trinity Observer
Tufts U	The Primary Source
UC Berkeley	The Berkeley Review
UC Davis	The Davis Republic
UC San Diego	The California Review

★paper shared by more than one campus

Conservative Campus Newspapers Affiliated With the Madison Center for Educational Affairs (page 2)

UC Santa Cruz	The Redwood Review
U of Chicago	The Whip
U of Dallas	The University Standard★
U of Florida	The Florida Review
U of Houston	The Houston Clarion
U of Illinois	The Orange & Blue Observer★
U of Kansas	The Oread Review
U of Massachusetts Amherst	The Minuteman
U of Michigan	The Michigan Review
U of North Carolina	The Carolina Critic
U of North Texas	The University Standard★
U of Northern Iowa	The UNI Sentinel
U of Oregon	The Oregon Commentator
U of Pennsylvania	The Red & Blue
U of South Carolina	The Carolina Spectator
U of Texas Arlington	The University Standard★
U of Texas Austin	The University Review
U of Virginia	The Virginia Advocate
U of Wisconsin Milwaukee	The UWM Times
Vanderbilt U	The Arena
Vassar College	The Vassar Spectator
Wake Forest U	The Wake Forest Critic
Washington & Lee U	The Washington & Lee Spectator
Wellesley College	Counterpoint★
Williams College	The Williams Free Press
Yale U	The Yale Free Press

★paper shared by more than one campus

[Source: Madison Center brochure, November 1996]

Youth Funding by Left-leaning Foundations

Foundation/ Funded Organizations	1995 Funding
Veatch Foundation	
US Student Association Foundation	$40,000
Student Environmental Action Coal.	$45,000
UNPLUG	$40,000
total	**$125,000**
Norman Foundation	
UNPLUG	$20,000
Student Environmental Action Coal.	$15,000
total	**$35,000**
List Foundation	
Center for Campus Organizing	$45,000
Green Corps	$15,000
Youth Action	$30,000
total	**$90,000**
Tides Foundation	
Students Organizing Students	$17,500
UNPLUG	$10,000
Student Environmental Action Coal.	$10,000
total	**$37,500**
Total funding for these organizations by four	
of the largest "youth politics" funders	**$287,500**

We inspected the 1995 annual reports of four large funders of progressive "youth politics" — The progressive funders gave less than $300,000 to national student and youth programs which encourage organizing and/or political participation, as opposed to community service. Examining the annual reports of the top four conservative funders influencing campus activism — Scaife, Olin, Bradley, and Carthage — we found a total of $3.8 million, or 13 times what progressive funders were giving.

Anti-Gay Organizations

from a list published by Political Research Associates, 1993

American Center for Law and Justice
American Family Association
American Freedom Coalition
Berean League
Christian Action Network
Christian Coalition
Christian Voice
Citizens for Excellence in Education
Coalition on Revival
Colorado for Family Values
Concerned Women for America
Coral Ridge Ministries
Council for National Policy
Eagle Forum
Exodus International
Family Life Ministries
Family Research Council
Focus on the Family
Free Congress Foundation
Inst. for the Scientific Investigation of Sexuality
Intercessors for America
John Birch Society
Liberty University
National Association of Christian Educators
National Citizens Action Network
National Legal Foundation
New Federalist
Oregon Citizens Alliance
Rockford Institute
Rutherford Insitute
Summit Ministries
Traditional Values Coalition

Pro-military Organizations

Aerospace Industries Association, DC
American Defense Institute, DC
American Defense Preparedness Association, VA (pub National Defense)
American Enterprise Institute, DC
American Foreign Policy Council, VA
American Legion (Boy's State, etc.), IN
American Security Council, DC
BU College of Comm. Program for the Study of Disinformation, MA
Center for National Security Studies, Los Alamos, CA
Center for Security Policy, DC
Center for Strategic and International Studies, DC
Center for Technical Studies in Security, Energy & Arms Control, CA
Coalition for Peace Through Strength, DC
Committee for the Free World, NY
Council for Interamerican Security, DC
Council for National Policy, DC
Defense Council Foundation
Eagle Forum, IL
Foreign Policy Research Institute, PA
Freedom House, NY
George C. Marshall Institute, DC or NY
Heritage Foundation, DC
High Frontier, DC
Hudson Institute , IN
Institute for Foreign Policy Analysis, MA
Institute for National Strategic Studies, DC
Institute of World Politics, DC
Institute on Terrorism and Subnational Conflict, DC
Jamestown Foundation, DC
National Security Industrial Association, DC
National Security Planning Associates, MA
National Strategy Forum, IL
National Strategy Information Center, DC
RAND Corporation, CA
Stanford University Hoover Institution, CA
US Global Strategy Council, DC
World Anti-Communist League (int'l org.)
World Affairs Council of Pittsburgh, VA
World Without War Council, NY
[Source: Center for Campus Organizing]

Sarah Mellon Scaife Foundation Grants to Universities, 1992

source: Foundation Grants Index supplement, March 1993

Boston U., Institute for the Study of Economic Culture	$125,000
California U. of PA, Government Contracting Assistance Program	$150,000
Carnegie-Mellon U., Center for the Study of Public Policy	$125,000
Claremont McKenna College, affirmative action/diversity study	$44,000
Clemson U. Foundation, Center for Policy Studies	$100,000
George Mason U., Center for Study of Public Choice	$132,000
George Mason U., Center for Study of Market Processes	$25,000
George Mason U., Law and Economics Center	$110,000
George Washington U., Insitute for Sino-Soviet Studies	$40,000
Johns Hopkins U., School for Advanced Studies	$75,000
Naval War C., Research Project	$25,000
New York U., Austrian economics program	$100,000
Pepperdine U., faculty chair in public policy	$250,000
Saint Vincent C., faculty development	$150,000
Smith C., Center for the Study of Social and Political Change	$75,000
Southwest Missouri State U., Ctr. for Defense & Strategic Studies	$85,000
Stanford U., Hoover Institution, various Depts.	$400,000
Tufts U., Fletcher School of Law and Diplomacy	$225,000
UCLA, Graduate School of Management	$100,000
U. of Chicago, Law and Economics Program	$125,000
U. of Connecticut, Research and Publication Support	$25,000
U. of Pittsburgh, Dept. of Economics	$104,000
U. of Pittsburgh, Ctr. for Res. on Contracts & the Structure of Enterprise	$100,000
U., Bradley Policy Research Center	$60,000
U. of S. Carolina, Graduate Research Assistantships and conference	$50,000
U. of Toronto, Fellowship for US political science grad students	$20,000
U. of Virginia Law School, Center for National Security Law	$300,000
Washington U., Center for the Study of American Business	$25,000

Note: This is the funding of only one Right-wing foundation for one year! Many of the other foundations that fund campus Right-wing organizing also fund Right-leaning academic programs.

Source Documents

Exhibit 1: Institute for Foreign Policy Analysis Funding
(see article on page 75)

```
                                                                FORM 990
          THE INSTITUTE FOR FOREIGN POLICY ANALYSIS, INC.       SCHEDULE A
                            6/30/91                             51-0192436
```

LIST OF CONTRIBUTORS IS NOT SUBJECT TO PUBLIC INSPECTION

PART IV - QUESTION 26(b) - CONTRIBUTIONS RECEIVED OVER FOUR-YEAR PERIOD IN
EXCESS OF 2% OF LINE 24 - COLUMN (e)

	TOTAL RECEIVED	LESS 2% OF TOTAL SUPPORT	EXCESS
Sarah Scaife Foundation 3900 Mellon Bank Building Pittsburgh, PA 15230	$1,305,000	$136,271	$1,168,729
Raytheon Company Missile Systems Division Hartwell Road Bedford, MA 01730	393,363	136,271	257,092
John M. Olin Foundation, Inc. 460 Park Avenue New York, NY 10022	576,763	136,271	440,492
Rockwell International Corp. 3370 Miraloma Avenue Anaheim, CA 92803	165,000	136,271	28,729
The Lynde and Harry Bradley Foundation 777 East Wisconsin Avenue Milwaukee, WI 52303	533,811	136,271	397,540

$2,292,582

EVIDENCE OF MILITARY AND RIGHT WING FUNDING OF NON_PROFIT
ORGANIZATION AFFILIATED WITH THE FLETCHER SCHOOL AT TUFTS U.

DIRECTOR ROBERT PFALTZGRAFF IS PAID OVER $150K in ADDITION TO
HIS SALARY AT TUFTS AS DIRECTOR OF THE NATIONAL SECURITY PROGRAM.

**The annual tax form for 1993 from the non-profit IFPA
show large contributions from weapons contractors such
as Raytheon and Rockwell corporation.**

Exhibit 2: US Funded Young Americas Foundation
(see description on page 40)

DONATIONS TOTALING OVER $36,522 since 1979

F.M. Kirby Foundation, Inc.
17 DeHart Street
Morristown, New Jersey 07960

1979	$10,000
1980	20,000
1981	50,000
Total 1979-81	$80,000

United States Information Agency
Fourth Street Southwest
Washington, D.C.   20547

1982	$ 36,386
1983	81,999
Total 1982-83	$118,385

FOUNDATIONS THAT GAVE $5,000 OR MORE IN 1983

Lakeview Fund, Inc.
Pleasantville, N.Y.   10570

Aug. 1983	$20,200

Adolph Coors Foundation
1434 New York Avenue N.W.
Suite 723
Washington, D.C.   20005

May 1983	$5,000

United States Information Agency
Fourth Street Southwest
Washington, D.C.   20547

Accum.	$81,999

IRS tax filings reveal government funding of the Young Americas Foundation by the US Information Agency in 1982 and 1983.

Exhibit 3: Young Americas Foundation Activities
(see description on page 40)

1984 correspondence from the Young Americas Foundation to the FBI, "exposing" CISPES as a terrorist group. This document was obtained by CISPES as part of a Freedom of Information Act request and lawsuit charging government disruption of lawful CISPES activities.

Index

DeBeauvoir, Simone, 48
Defense Council Foundation, 118
Defense Nuclear Agency, 77
Defense Policy and Arms Control, 78
defunding of progressive groups, vi, 8-9
    14-15, 36, 37, 61
DeLay, Tom (R-Tex.), 73
Department of Defense (DOD), 80, 90
Department of the Navy, 77
Detlefsen, Robert, 42
DIversity and Division, 68
Dobson, James, 9
Doolittle, John (R-Calif), 74
Draper, Mark, 12, 35
Duke University, 7, 51, 55, 114
Duke, David, 7
DuPont, Pierre, 44

Eagle Eye, 14
Eagle Forum Collegians, The (EFC), 8,
    14, 37, 47-50, 110
Eagle Forum Legal Defense & Education
    Fund, 34, 37, 117, 118
Earhart Foundation, 113
Edison Electic Institiute, 72
Education and Research Institute, The
    (ERI), 34, 40, 110
Encyclopedia of Associations , 92
Equal Employment Opportunity
    Commission (EEOC), 98
Every Student's Choice, 13
Executive Intelligence Review, 110
Exodus International (EI), 13, 117
Exxon, 73

F. M. Kirby Foundation, 113
Fallout, the Leading Voice in Student
    Radio, 110
False Memory Syndrome Foundation,
    110
Faludi, Susan, 62
Family Life Ministries, 117
Family Research Council, 117
FBI, 6
Federalist Society, 34, 37, 111
Feminist Majority, 24
Feminists for Life, 110
Filene, Edward, 94
firing, 9, 60
First Amendment Coalition, 3, 111

Flanders, Laura, 64
Fleming, Thomas, 69
Fletcher School of Law and Diplomacy,
    77, 79
Florida State University, 114
Focus on the Family, 117
Forbes, Steve, 49
Foreign Policy Research Institute, 118
Foundation Center, 90
Foundation for Economic Education,
    111
Foundation Grants Index, 90, 92
Free Congress Foundation, 42, 111, 117
Freedom House, 118
Freedom of Information Act (FOIA),
    90, 97
Friedan, Betty, 48
Frishberg, Ivan, 30, 32
FSEOG, 30
Fund for American Studies, 111
Fund, John, 40

G.T.E. Corporation, 77
Gaffney, Frank Jr., 47-48
Galli, Joe, 29
George C. Marshall Institute, 118
George Washington University, 44
Georgetown University, 39, 49, 114
German Coal Mining Association, 72-73
Gingrich, Newt, vii, 2, 28-29, 41, 44,
    53
Ginsburg, Ruth Bader, 48
Glick, Brian, 87
Goldwater, Barry, 41, 47
Gramm, Phil, 47
Greve, Michael, 18, 41
Grove City College, 112
Grover Hermann Foundation, 113

Hart, Ben, 42
Harvard U, 114
Hassett, Jody, 40
Hees, Peter, 37
Helm, Jesse, 67
Henry Salvatori Foundation, 34, 113
Herber, Robert, 79
Heritage Foundation, The (HF), 42, 49,
    66, 79, 111, 118
Heterodoxy, 36, 111
High Frontier, 118

Ludwig Von Mises Institute, 111
Lukefahr, Robert, 40
Lynde & Harry Bradley Foundation, 113
Lynde and Harry Bradley Foundation, 34
Lynn, Barry W., 18

M. J. Murdock Charitable Trust, 113
Madison Center for Educational Affairs, 3, 38, 40, 55, 56, 111
Martin, Jerry, 52
Massachusetts Association of Scholars, 39
Matalin, Mary, 63
McDonald, Michael, 41
McDonnell Douglas, 77
McGuire, Patricia, 52
McGurn, Bill, 40
McKeon, Howard P. (R-CA) , 31
McWhiney, Grady, 69
Meese, Ed, 44
Miami University, 114
Michaels, Pat, 71-73
Michigan State University, 8
Missouri Public interest Research Group (MoPIRG), 8
MIT, 45, 75-6, 96, 114
Mitchell, Robert, 56
MITRE Corporation, 76
Montana College of Mineral Science and Technology, 60
Montgomery Street Foundation, 113
Moon, Rev. Sun Myung, 73
Morehouse College, 11
Mountain States Legal Foundation, 112
Mt. Holyoke, 51
Multicultural Student's Guide to Colleges, 57

NAS Update, 39
Natinal Gay and Lesbian Task Force Policy Institute, 13
National Alliance, 111
National Alumni Forum (NAF), 34, 39, 52-3
National Alumni Foundation (NAF), 51
National Association for the Advancement of White People, 111
National Association of Christian Educators, 117

National Association of Scholars (NAS), 34, 39, 111
National Citizens Action Network, 117
National Defense University, 112
National Empowerment Television, 111
National Endowment for the Humanitites, 52
National Journalism Center see The Education and Research Institute,
National Legal Foundation, 117
National Minority Politics, 68
National Right to Work Committee, 79
National Science Board, 98
National Security Council, 78, 79
National Security Industrial Association, 118
National Security Planning Associates, 79, 118
National Strategy Forum, 118
National Strategy Information Center, 118
National Traditionalist Caucus, 111
National Women's Studies Association, 9
Naval War College, 79
New England Legal Foundation, 112
New Federalist, 117
New York University, 8
newspaper ads, vii, 12-13,
Nixon, Richard M., 78
Northern Arizona University, 14
North Carolina State University, 114
North, Oliver, 41, 44, 49
Northeastern Illinois University, 7
Northern Arizona University, 8
Northwestern University, 8, 9, 114
Notre Dame, 61, 114
Nunn, Sam, 78

O'Conner, Supreme Court Justice, 37
Oberlin College, 114
Ohio State University, 7
Oregon Citizens Alliance, 117

Pacific Legal Foundation, 112
Pacific Research Institue, 73
Parker, J.A., 66
Parker, Star, 66-67
PC see Political Correctness,
Pell Grant Program, 30

Resources Available From the Center for Campus Organizing

In addition to monitoring the campus Right, CCO serves as a clearinghouse providing access to skills, resources, and allies for all kinds of progressive organizations and progressive newspapers on college campuses.

You can obtain more information on many of the services below by consulting our web site at **http://www.cco.org** .

Campus Organizing Resources — CCO's activist resource library features books, guides and pamphlets to help campus activists be more successful and informed. The *Campus Organizing Guide for Peace and Justice Groups* is a basic 16-page guide to campus organizing, available in bulk for only 25¢ a copy; we also have a guides to planning a speaking event, creative actions, and 30 different alerts introducing on student activist issues such as:

Abortion Access	Financial Aid Cuts
Academic Racism	Gay, Lesbian, Bi Organizing
Animal Rights	Haiti
Anti-Immigrant Racism	Korea
Anti-Slavery	Military Spending
Bosnia	ROTC Off Campus
Burma	Stopping Fraternity Abuse
Campaign Finance	Tibet
Corporate Power	Violence Against Women
Feminist Organizing	

Organizing advice — CCO staff are always available by phone or e-mail to answer questions and share resources on any aspect of campus organizing or alternative journalism. If we can't answer your question, we can refer you to someone who can.

CANET — a free e-mail network for campus activists, with topics such as education rights, feminism, poverty, anti-racism, monitoring the right, etc. For information send e-mail to canet-info@pencil.math.missouri.edu.

Infusion — a quarterly newsletter providing "tools for action and education" for people interested in campus activism.

Outreach and Training — experienced campus organizers are available, for a small fee, to go to your campus and provide training to area activists.

Campus Alternative Journalism Program (CAJP)

CCO's CAJP provides journalism resources to a growing network of over 90 campus alternative publications. We provide a comprehensive 160-page guide to creating your own campus newspaper, *Afflict the Comfortable, Comfort the Afflicted,* as well as a guide to obtaining an internship in the alternative campus press.

The CAJP network also connects campus papers and student alternative journalists to share articles, ideas and technical assistance. We plan regional meetings for campus journalists and provide a free e-mail article exchange (CAN-EX).

Please consider becoming a member of CCO. Our programs help campus activists develop organizing skills, create alternative media, and link up with national groups. We encourage long-term political commitment, so that young activists will develop into lifelong community organizers and progressive journalists. Your contribution to CCO today can help build the social justice movements of the next century!

Center for Campus Organizing, Box 748, Cambridge, MA 02142
Tel. (617) 354-9363 • Fax (617) 547-5067 • cco@igc.apc.org

Return to CCO, Box 748, Cambridge, MA 02142

Name_____

Phone (s)_____ School_____

Address_____

City_____ State_____ Zip_____

Campus Group_____

Please send me:

__a CCO brochure & full publacations list

__info on CCO's internship program

__info on being a Faculty Campus Contact

__info on starting an alternative newspaper

__info on hosting a student activist training

I want to order:

qty		Price
___ Organizing Guides @ $1		___
___ 50 Org. Guides @ $15		___
___ Uncovering the Right @ $10		___
___ 5 Right Guides @ $25		___

Total (prices include shipping): $_____

I want to support campus peace and justice organizing by:

__Enclosing a tax-deductible donation to CCO of: $_____

__Subscribing to *Infusion*, the quarterly newsletter of the Center $_____
    for Campus Organizing ($25 reg., $10 student and low income)

Please make checks payable to "Center for Campus Organizing." The portion of any donation over $10 is tax-deductible.

About the Authors

Chip Berlet is a staff member at Political Research Associates in Somerville, MA.

Erin Bush was an intern for CCO's precursor, the University Conversion Project, in the summer of 1992.

Rich Cowan is founder of the Center for Campus Organizing. He recieved bachelor's and master's degrees in Computer Science from M.I.T. in 1987. He has over 10 years of organizing experience with student and community groups, and spearheaded the National Day of Campus Action on America in 1995.

Sara Diamond is the author of several books on right-wing movements including *Spiritual Warfare*, and lives in California.

Theo Emery is a free-lance writer living in Boston, MA.

Harley Gambill is a sophomore at Antioch College in Ohio and was an intern for CCO in the summer of 1997.

Ross Gelbspan is a former reporter from the Boston Globe.

Sonya Huber is the director of the Campus Alternative Journalism Project and editor of CCO's newsletter, *Infusion*.

John Keeble is a freelance writer.

David Kennedy wrote for *Perspective: Harvard's Monthly Jounral of Liberal Opinion*.

Michael Kennedy attended Villanova University majoring in Peace Studies.

Ben Leon is a senior at Antioch College in Ohio and was an intern for CCO in 1997.

Dalya Massachi recently received a Master's Degree in Journalism and Development at Ohio University, and worked on the predecessor publication to this guide.

Nicole Newton is a senior at Michigan State University and is a former staff person at the Center for Campus Organizing.

Jennifer Pozner attended Hampshire College and is a former member of the CCO staff.

Nari Rhee is a graduate student at the University of California at Irvine and was an intern for CCO in the summer of 1996.

Justin Roberts attends Whittenburg University and was an intern for CCO in the summer of 1996.

Ami Roeder is a 1996 graduate of Antioch College and was an intern and consultant to CCO during 1996.

Jeremy Smith is a former staff person at CCO who is now a member of the Board of Directors.

Nova Ren Suma recently graduated from Antioch College in Ohio and was an intern for CCO in the summer of 1996.

John K. Wilson is a graduate student at the University of Chicago and is active is Teachers for a Democratic Culture. He works on the *Unitveristy of Chicago Free Press* and *Chicago Ink*.